365
Prayers
For
Your Husband

365
Prayers
For
Your Husband

Empower Your Prayers with the Word

Daily Scriptures and Prayers

to Lift Up Your Husband or Future Husband

Monique O'Neal, MEd, LPCC

Published by Divine Interventions, LLC

ISBN: 9798385682584
Printed in the United States of America

Contents

DEDICATION

To My Dear Husband Brandon, I am honored that God chose you for me and me for you. Thank you for being obedient to the leading of Christ, choosing me, loving me, and giving me the greatest gifts, our sons. We went from being classmates and riding the same school bus, from the first grade to the ninth grade. Who would have known that our lives would circle back around to complete God's will for our lives? That is just like God, isn't it? You are a mighty man of Valor and I honor you. I love you, babe.

"...and the two will become one flesh."

(Mark 10:8, NIV)

x

INTRODUCTION

If you are a new wife, looking to be married, or have been married for half a century, this book is for you. Brandon and I have been married for thirteen years, log enough to understand the importance of praying for your spouse.

All marriages will go through seasons of happiness and seasons that are difficult. It is not always spring, summer, lilies, and daisies. You will go through times of shedding, dry and wintery mixes. It is in these tough times and seasons that I have found the power of prayer to be so effective.

Sometimes you will not know what to pray for because your husband is not going to always discuss with you the sentiments of his heart. Whether he requests it or not, we are to keep him always covered in prayer. You are the closest person on earth to him. God has chosen you to be his helper, "lookout," and support. This book was designed with that in mind.

I want you to know that this book was an act of obedience, inspired by the Holy Spirit because God wanted you to have a tool to undergird your husband consistently. I believe that in the days ahead, choosing to pray for your husband, or future husband, you will be praying for the very thing he might be needing at that moment.

This book has a bible verse (365 different scriptures) for every single day of the year that will guide you in praying the Word of God over your husband. Just think of the promises connected to His Word that you are speaking over your husband becoming activated in your lives. Remember, His Word, *"will not return to me empty" (Isaiah 55:11, NIV), "but will accomplish what I desire and achieve the purpose for which I sent it."*

While you are reading scripture and praying for your husband, I encourage you to make it personal by saying your husband's name wherever you see *"my husband."*

If you are still waiting to be married, speak in faith, and replace *"my husband"* with *"my future husband.*" You're choosing to pray for your future husband in advance as an act of faith. This is letting God know that you are believing that he is on the way! What a blessing to be able to pray for the man God has for you, even if you have not met him yet.

Consistently in these prayers, you will see, "Lord, I thank You for my husband…" You may not see all the characteristics present in your husband that you are thanking God for, but make it a practice to thank God in advance for what He is going to do in the life of your husband. We are praying to *the God who gives life to the dead and calls into being things that were not (Romans 4:17, NIV)."* Your life is voice-activated, exercise your authority to speak those things into existence.

Although this book is in a daily format, it is not a race to the finish line. If there is a particular prayer or maybe some prayers that resonate with you, stop, meditate, and pray fervently for your husband. The word declares that *"the effectual, fervent prayer of a righteous man (woman) availeth much (James 5:16, KJV)."* Petition the Lord for your husband's love, grace, growth, and life in Him.

In this book, you will find prayers just for you, the wife. We do not ever want to be presumptuous in thinking that we have it all together. You want to make sure that your heart is positioned right as you go before the Lord in prayer. Recognize that this is not an attempt to "fix" your husband. Instead, you are praying the Word of God to cover him in the Love of God.

My prayer is that this book will become a source of blessing and encouragement to you, your spouse, and those waiting to be married. May it bring comfort to the hurting, hope to the believing, and joy to the sorrowful. May it also strengthen your faith as you look to God to transform the life of your husband. May it draw you closer to God and help you and your current or future husband experience the fullness of God's love and grace.

JANUARY

January 1

"Oh, the joys of those who do not follow the advice of the wicked, or stand around with sinners, or join in with mockers." **(Psalm 1:1)**

Dear Lord, thank you for giving my husband the confidence to not entertain the advice of the wicked. Thank you that he takes no pleasure in hanging out with sinners. Thank you that he does not join in with mockers. Lead him to walk uprightly with you Lord. Protect him from the temptation of the world and help him to stay true to your ways. Give him the wisdom to discern what is right and just, and the strength to stand firm in his beliefs. Help him to grow in his faith and be a light to those around him. Thank you for your unfailing love and your promises to those who seek you. I trust that you will guide and protect my husband every step of the way.

In the name of Jesus, I pray, Amen.

January 2

"But they delight in the law of the Lord, meditating on it day and night." **(Psalm 1:2)**

Dear Lord, thank you that my husband loves your Word and takes delight in your laws and decrees. Thank you, Lord, that he finds pleasure in meditating on your Word both day and night and that he does not meditate on the wrong things. I pray to God that you would block any distractions that would tempt him to meditate on anything other than the truth or your Word.

In the name of Jesus, I pray, Amen.

January 3

"They are like trees planted along the riverbank, bearing fruit each season. Their leaves never wither, and they prosper in all they do." **(Psalm 1:3)**

Dear Lord, I thank you that my husband is a man of God that bears fruit. I thank you that his leaves do not wither and that he prospers in all that he does. Bless his hands as he works. Bless his heart as he loves. Bless his finances as he works with integrity. Bless his going out and his coming in. Bless his health efforts, to take care of his body. Bless him with wisdom and care to love his family the way you have called him to love.

In the name of Jesus, I pray, Amen.

January 4

"For the Lord watches over the path of the godly, but the path of the wicked leads to destruction." **(Psalm 1:6)**

Dear Lord, I ask that you continue to guide my husband on the path of righteousness and bless him with your wisdom, strength, and discernment. I pray he always seeks your will in his life and follows your commandments. Protect him from the ways of the wicked and surround him with your love and grace. Help him to grow in faith and become the man that you have called him to be.

In the name of Jesus, I pray, Amen.

January 5

"And He said to me, "My grace is sufficient for you, for My strength is made perfect in weakness." Therefore most gladly I will rather boast in my infirmities, that the power of Christ may rest upon me.
Therefore I take pleasure in infirmities, in reproaches, in needs, in persecutions, in distresses, for Christ's sake. For when I am weak, then I am strong."
(2 Corinthians 12:9-10)

Dear Lord, thank you for your grace and strength that is made perfect in my husband's weakness. Help him to not be ashamed of his weakness, but to take pleasure in his infirmities, reproaches, needs, persecutions, and distresses for your sake. Give him a fresh perspective to lean on you in times of weakness. Teach him to naturally rely on you and not his strength. Remind him that when he feels weak, his strength is made perfect in you and only you.

In the name of Jesus, I pray, Amen.

January 6

"Yet in all these things we are more than conquerors through Him who loved us." **(Romans 8:37)**

Dear Lord, give my husband supernatural strength to conquer whatever fears and concerns he has on his mind today. Allow your Holy Spirit to arise in him to remind him that he is More than a Conqueror because he has you. Strengthen him with your power, fill him with your courage, and give him the endurance to overcome any obstacle that comes his way. I pray he walks in confidence, knowing that he is loved and empowered by you. I pray that you continue to bless him in all aspects of his life and use him as a vessel to glorify Your name.

In the name of Jesus, I pray, Amen.

January 7

"And the peace of God, which surpasses all understanding, will guard your hearts and minds through Christ Jesus." **(Philippians 4:7)**

Dear Lord, I thank you for your peace that rests on and within my husband. I pray that your peace consumes his understanding and misunderstandings and any irrational thoughts that he may hold. Lord, reverse any irrational thoughts or lies he may believe and give him a godly perspective. God, I pray that you illuminate your truth in his mind. Blot out any other inconsistencies or distractions that the enemy sends. Thank you for a husband that looks to you to guard his heart and mind.

In the name of Jesus, I pray, Amen.

January 8

*"Create in me a clean heart, O God, And renew a stead-fast spirit within me." (**Psalm 51:10**)*

Dear Lord, thank you for renewing steadfastness with-in my husband and that you are creating in him a clean heart. Heal him from past hurts. Reveal to him any unforgiveness and bitterness that he may be car-rying. Please help him to overcome any temptations or struggles he may be facing and give him the strength and courage to persevere. I pray that you will bless him with your love, grace, and mercy and that he may always find renewed joy and peace in your presence. Thank you for revealing what needs to be revealed for him to obtain a clean heart.

In the name of Jesus, I pray, Amen.

January 9

"Teach me Your way, O Lord; I will walk in Your truth; Unite my heart to fear Your name." (Psalm 86:11)

Dear Lord, I thank you Lord that I have a husband that walks in your truth and that he reveres your name in his heart. Give him an undivided heart, that he may fear your name. I pray he always has a heart that pursues after you and desires to do your will. Help him to trust in your goodness and your faithfulness, even in times of trial and difficulty. Fill his heart with your peace and let your love guide his steps. I pray that he will continue to grow in his relationship with you and that you will bless him with wisdom, strength, and grace.

In the name of Jesus, I pray, Amen.

January 10

*"A good man out of the good treasure of his heart brings forth good; and an evil man out of the evil [a]treasure of his heart brings forth evil. For out of the abundance of the heart his mouth speaks." (**Luke 6:45**)*

Dear Lord, I thank you for a husband who brings forth good out of the good treasure of his heart. Fill his heart every day with your Love, even when he does not know he needs it. Teach him how to love others from the love that you show. Thank you that his mouth speaks good things and that he is a man of God that speaks life over himself and our family.

In the name of Jesus, I pray, Amen.

January 11

"The heart is deceitful above all things, And desperately wicked; Who can know it? I, the Lord, search the heart, I test the mind, Even to give every man according to his ways, According to the fruit of his doings."
(Jeremiah 17:9-10)

Dear Lord, I pray for my husband and me, asking that you would search our hearts and know our thoughts, just as it says in Jeremiah 17:9-10. Reveal to us any areas where we may be struggling, any attitudes or behaviors that are not pleasing to you, and any ways in which we may be deceiving ourselves. Help us to fully surrender our hearts and our lives to you, trusting in your guidance and your love. May you bless our marriage with your grace and your peace, and may we always seek to honor you in all that we do. Thank you, God, for your unfailing love and your faithful presence in our lives.

In the name of Jesus, I pray, Amen.

January 12

"Let not your heart be troubled; you believe in God, believe also in Me." (John 14:1)

Dear Lord Jesus, show my husband your face. Comfort his troubled heart. Calm any anxieties or worries that may be weighing on his heart. Help him to trust in your love and your goodness. Let him look to you and nothing else {insert his weakness, alcohol, drugs, food, sexual perversion, gambling, insecurity, violence} when his heart is troubled. Jesus, remind him that he can run to you. And I pray he finds comfort and strength in your presence, and I pray he feels your loving arms around him. Lord Jesus, block the plans of the enemy designed to distract him. Help him to be a loving and supportive husband, and may our marriage always be rooted and grounded in your truth and your love. Thank you, God, for your constant care and your never-ending grace.

In the name of Jesus, I pray, Amen.

January 13

*"And made no distinction between us and them, purifying their hearts by faith." (**Acts 15:9**)*

Lord Jesus, thank You for not making a distinction between us and them and granting us the same love, power, and promises to anyone who believes in you and accepts you as their Lord. Please help my husband to fully embrace this truth, knowing that he is acceptable and loved by you regardless of his background or his past mistakes. Help him to walk in the freedom of your forgiveness and to live a life that honors and glorifies you. And as he grasps the depths of your love for him, may his life be a testimony to your amazing grace. Thank you, God, for your unconditional love and your never-ending mercy.

In the name of Jesus, I pray, Amen.

January 14

"But your iniquities have separated you from your God; And your sins have hidden His face from you, So that He will not hear." (Isaiah 59:2)

Dear Lord Jesus, thank you for dying on the cross and forgiving us for all our sins; past, present, and future. I pray that as my husband seeks your face, you would make known iniquities in his life so that he is not separated from you. Hide not your face from him. Hear his prayers oh God. Hear my prayer and forgive me of all sin and iniquities in my life and my family line. Forgive my husband and his family line of generational sin and iniquity. Let it stop with us! Lord, I thank you and receive your forgiveness!

In the name of Jesus, I pray, Amen.

January 15

"There is no soundness in my flesh.
Because of Your anger, Nor any health in my bones be-
cause of my sin. For my iniquities have gone over my
head; Like a heavy burden they are too heavy for me."
(Psalm 38:3-4)

Dear Lord Jesus, thank you that my husband has good health. In the name of Jesus, remove any pain or illness that he may be experiencing. Lift him, and restore him to full health, both physically and emotionally. I pray he finds comfort in your presence and in the knowledge that you are with him through every trial and difficulty. If there is any sin in his life blocking his wellness, please reveal it. Your word says that you were wounded for our transgressions, bruised for our iniquities; the chastisement of our peace was upon you, and with your stripes, we are healed! Thank you for being a God that forgives us of all our sins and heals all our diseases! I declare Lord, you are a good, good Father.

In the name of Jesus, I pray, Amen.

January 16

"Beloved, if our heart does not convict us [of guilt], we have confidence [complete assurance and boldness] before God; and we receive from Him whatever we ask because we [carefully and consistently] keep His commandments and do the things that are pleasing in His sight [habitually seeking to follow His plan for us]."
(I John 3:21-22)

Dear Lord, give my husband complete assurance and boldness in you. Thank you for a husband who not only keeps your commands, but loves to keep your commands, and does those things that are pleasing in your sight. What a man! Thank you, Lord! Remind this mighty man that he can approach you with boldness and receive whatever he asks for according to your will. Give him peace and assurance in the knowledge of your unfailing love and remind him that his life has purpose and value.

In the name of Jesus, I pray, Amen.

January 17

"He who covers his sins will not prosper, but whoever confesses and forsakes them will have mercy."
(Proverbs 28:13)

Dear Lord, I pray for my husband today and thank you for his life. I thank you that he is not a man that covers his sins, but he is a man that humbly confesses his sins. Thank you for your example of humility and that he takes his walk with Christ seriously. Because of this, your word declares that whatever he does prospers. Thank you for your Holy Spirit and your goodness that leads my husband to repentance, confessions, and the forsaking of his sins. Remove any shame connected to sin that he is tempted to cover. Remind him that there is no condemnation because he is yours. Thank you for mercy, Father.

In the name of Jesus, I pray, Amen.

January 18

"And let the beauty of the Lord our God be upon us And establish the work of our hands for us; Yes, establish the work of our hands." (Psalm 90:17)

Dear Lord, I come before you today in prayer with a heart full of love for my dear husband. I ask that you bless the work of his hands and guide him in all his endeavors. May the efforts he puts forth be fruitful and productive, bringing glory and honor to your name. I pray that he always feels your presence and guidance in his work and profession. I pray that you would continue to bless him and use him for your purposes and your glory. Lord, let your beauty shine in and through my husband. Give him divine insight and creativity. Let his work "stand out" from his colleagues. Grant him favor with you Lord, and favor with men.

In the name of Jesus, I pray, Amen.

January 19

"But the wisdom that is from above is first pure, then peaceable, gentle, willing to yield, full of mercy and good fruits, without partiality and without hypocrisy."
(James 3:17)

Dear Lord, I praise you for a husband who is peaceful, gentle, willing to yield, full of mercy, and good fruits. I pray he demonstrates the fruit of the Spirit, love, joy, peace, patience, kindness, goodness, gentleness, faithfulness, and self-control in his life, in our marriage, and our home. Thank you that he does not view these characteristics as a sign of weakness, but as Godly character to attain. Lord, I praise you that his lifestyle matches his lip service. He lives the life he speaks about. Thank you, Father.

In the name of Jesus, I pray, Amen.

January 20

*"My son, do not forget my law, But let your heart keep my commands; For length of days and long life and peace they will add to you." **(Proverbs 3:1-2)***

Dear Lord, I come to you today thankful that You have blessed my husband with a long life. I declare and decree that he will live and not die; and that he will declare the works of the Lord, in the land of the living.

Thank you that this life is full of peace because his heart keeps your commands. I pray he find pleasure in remembering and keeping your Word in his heart.

In the name of Jesus, I pray, Amen.

January 21

"Happy is the man who finds wisdom, And the man who gains understanding;" **(Proverbs 3: 13)**

Dear Lord, I pray for a happy husband. I pray that he is so full of you, that he exudes love and joy unspeakable. Lead him to find wisdom, increasing his understanding in the matters of life and of this world. Let his motives stem from the righteous desire to obtain your understanding and not from a desire to just "be right." Thank you that his happiness, wisdom, and understanding resonate through our home, resulting in peace and resolution.

In the name of Jesus, I pray, Amen.

January 22

"Put away from you a deceitful mouth, And put perverse lips far from you." **(Proverbs 4:24)**

Dear Lord, today I am asking for your guidance and protection over my husband's words and actions. Help him to be intentional about the words he speaks, and may they always be words of truth, love, and kindness that build up those around him. Protect him from any negative influences that may tempt him to have perverse speech and a deceitful mouth. Give him the discernment to know right from wrong. I pray he always looks for wisdom and understanding, and may his heart be filled with a desire to live a life that is pleasing to you.

In the name of Jesus, I pray, Amen.

January 23

"Let your eyes look straight ahead, And your eyelids look right before you." **(Proverbs 4:25)**

Dear Lord, thank you for the gift of my husband, and I pray that today and always, you would continue to bless him and use him for your purposes. Lord, grant my husband tunnel vision for the things of God. Thank you for keeping his eyes focused on the things right before him. Give him strength and wisdom to not become distracted by the things of the world, the lust of the eye, the lust of the flesh, and the pride of life.

In the name of Jesus, I pray, Amen.

January 24

"My wounds are foul and festering because of my foolish-ness." (Psalm 38:5)

Dear Lord, I ask that you forgive my husband for any wrongs he has committed and heal him from the inside out. May your grace and mercy pour out upon him, bringing him comfort and relief. Help him to turn away from any foolishness or sin in his life and guide him towards a path of righteousness and obedience to you. Give him strength and discipline in you to not entertain the foolishness of his flesh. The flesh is weak, but Lord, you are mighty! Lead him to tap into the power that is in your Name.

In the name of Jesus, I pray, Amen.

January 25

"But God raised Him up, releasing Him and bringing an end to the agony of death, since it was impossible for Him to be held in death's power." (Acts 2:24)

Heavenly Father, you have won the victory! You brought an end to the agony of death. Thank you, Father, for the victory that we have through your son Jesus Christ. Lord, today I pray that my husband would always remember the power of your resurrection and the hope that we have in you. Help him to walk in the victory that you have already won for us and to trust in your faithfulness and goodness, no matter what. It was impossible for Jesus "to be held in death's power." That means that nothing is impossible when you are involved! Help my husband to tap into and take advantage of the resurrection power that lies within.

In the name of Jesus, I pray, Amen.

January 26

"I will instruct you and teach you in the way you should go: I will counsel you with my eye upon you."
(Psalm 32:8)

Dear Lord, thank you for your instruction. Thank you to the Holy Spirit, who is a guide. Thank you for teaching my husband the way he should go. Thank you for having his best interest at heart, for counseling him, and for keeping your eye on him. I pray that you would open his ears to hear your voice and his heart to receive your wisdom. Help him to trust in your leading and to follow your path, even when it may not be easy or clear. Thank you for your faithful love and guidance in his life.

In the name of Jesus, I pray, Amen.

January 27

"For ye were sometimes darkness, but now are ye light in the Lord: walk as children of light." **(Ephesians 5:8)**

Dear Lord, I come before you today with a grateful heart for the salvation that you have given us through your Son, Jesus Christ. Your Word tells us that we were once in darkness, but now we are children of light in the Lord. I praise you that my husband no longer walks in darkness but is now walking in the light with You. Thank you that he turns from evil and chooses to live for You, daily. I pray that you would continue to transform my husband into the image of your Son and help him to live a life that reflects your light to those around him. May his words, actions, and attitudes be pleasing to you and may they draw others to you. Thank you for the gift of your grace and the joy that comes from walking in your light.

In the name of Jesus, I pray, Amen.

January 28

"Therefore, see that you walk carefully [living life with honor, purpose, and courage; shunning those who tolerate and enable evil], not as the unwise, but as wise [sensible, intelligent, discerning people],"
(Ephesians 5:15)

Dear Lord, I pray that my husband would walk in wisdom, honor, and purpose. Succeeding at every opportunity that you bring his way. I pray he be discerning and seek your will in all his decisions, actions, and interactions. I pray that he would be intentional in his relationships and invest his time and energy in things that truly matter. Help him to be a good steward of the resources you have given him and to use them for your glory. I pray he be a shining light in this world, reflecting your love and truth to those around him. Thank you for your grace and your constant presence in his life.

In the name of Jesus, I pray, Amen.

January 29

"From the fruit of their lips people are filled with good things, and the work of their hands brings them reward."
(Proverbs 12:14)

Dear Lord, I come before you humbly today to say thank you! Thank you for choosing me to love the man of God you have created for me. Thank you for choosing him to love me like you love the church. I pray today that you would help him to use his tongue to build himself, to build me, and others up and not to tear down, to encourage and not to discourage, and to speak with kindness and love. I pray that he would continue to seek your wisdom and guidance in all his conversations and interactions. I pray that the work of my husband's hands brings him reward, spiritually, naturally, and financially. Continue to teach him to speak the Word from the fruit of his lips so that he might become filled with good things and pour into those around him.

In the name of Jesus, I pray, Amen.

January 30

"The righteous man walks in his integrity; His children are blessed after him." (Proverbs 20:7)

Dear Lord, I thank you that my husband walks in integrity and honor before you and others. I pray he always strives to live a blameless life and be a man of righteousness. I pray that you would guide him in all his ways and help him to make wise choices that bring glory to your name. Lord, I pray that he be a man of his word, keeping his promises and treating others with respect and kindness. I pray that he would be a light in this world, reflecting your truth and love to those around him. Thank you that all our children and children to come will become blessed after and because of him. Thank you for your grace and your constant presence in his life.

In the name of Jesus, I pray, Amen.

January 31

*"How enriched are they who find their strength in the
Lord; within their hearts are the highways of holiness!"*
(Psalm 84:5)

Dear Lord, I pray that my husband would find his
strength and refreshing in you alone. I pray he recognize in your presence is where true joy and fulfillment
exist. Help him to have a deep desire to dwell in your
house and to seek you daily. I pray he find his home in
you and the blessings of your favor and protection. I
pray that by your spirit he would continue to grow
strong in faith. I pray he be a source of encouragement
and hope to those around him, reflecting your love
and grace. Thank you for your unending goodness and
mercy.

In the name of Jesus, I pray, Amen.

FEBRUARY

February 1

*"For the Lord God is a sun and shield;" **(Psalm 84:11a)***

Dear Lord, thank you for being the sun and shield in my husband's life. Thank you for being the light that he needs to find his way and thank you for being the light that shines through him. Thank you for the warmth he feels from your love. May it envelop him today. Thank you for being his protector. Thank you for protecting him from the fiery darts of the enemy. I pray he has sweet rest, knowing that you are his sun and shield and everything he needs is in you. You go before him; you are right beside him and behind him. I pray he feels that protection today.

In the name of Jesus, I pray, Amen.

February 2

"The Lord will give grace and glory; No good thing will He withhold From those who walk uprightly."
(Psalm 84:11b)

Dear Lord, I pray for grace and glory to surround my husband. Thank you that he is a man that walks uprightly. Your word says that no good thing will you withhold from those who walk uprightly, so I pray that he would experience your goodness and provision in his life. I pray that my husband will trust in your promise. Help him to have faith in your provision, even when he may not see it. I pray he finds comfort in knowing that you have a plan for his life and that you are working all things together for his good. I pray he continues to seek you and your will for his life, knowing that you have good things in store for him.

In the name of Jesus, I pray, Amen.

February 3

*"My son, give attention to my words; Incline your ear to my sayings." (**Proverbs 4:20**)*

Dear Lord, your word is a lamp to our feet and a light unto our paths. It leads and directs us in the way that we should go. I thank you Lord for a husband that pays close attention to your words. I pray he always listens to your teachings and never let them depart from his hearing. May his ears be attentive to your wisdom, and I pray he inclines his heart to understanding. Please bless him with a discerning heart and help him to make wise choices that honor you. Thank you for your constant love and guidance.

In the name of Jesus, I pray, Amen.

February 4

"Now the fruit of righteousness is sown in peace by those who make peace." (James 3:18)

Dear Lord, you are the ultimate peace giver. I thank you for your peace that surpasses all our understanding. I thank you Lord for a peace-making husband. Because he is a peacemaker, his mind is at peace. Therefore, I declare and decree that my husband will exude peace. Our home is full of peace. Our marriage will be full of peace. Lord, we welcome your reconciling peace to our covenant relationship with you. Lord, I thank you for the righteousness that is the fruit that we see from his life. Thank you for his leadership and his example of peace in our home.

In the name of Jesus, I pray, Amen.

February 5

"Go from the presence of a foolish man, when you do not perceive in him the lips of knowledge." **(Proverbs 14:7)**

Dear Lord, keep my husband from foolish men. Help him to be discerning and to surround himself with wise counsel. I pray he seeks your guidance and wisdom in all that he does and has a heart that is open to correction and growth. Lord, I pray that he would be a man of character, and integrity and that he would speak words that are full of wisdom and grace. Thank you for sending men into his life that encourage, empower, and challenge him to be the man of God you have called him to be.

In the name of Jesus, I pray, Amen.

February 6

"Do nothing out of selfish ambition or vain conceit. Rather, in humility value others above yourselves, not looking to your own interests but each of you to the interests of the others." **(Philippians 2:3-4)**

Heavenly Father, thank you for your love. Thank you for your love that is made manifest in my husband's life. Because you are love, and you loved us first, we have an example of humility in love. I thank you that my husband is a selfless man. He is humble and inclined to serve others above himself. I thank you for the example of selfless love that he models/will model in our marriage, and in our home. I declare and decree that love, humility, selflessness, and peace will flow through our home and marriage.

In the name of Jesus, I pray, Amen.

February 7

"I will behave wisely in a perfect way. Oh, when will You come to me? I will walk within my house with a perfect heart." (Psalm 101:2)

Dear Lord, I come to you today on behalf of my husband and ask that you would give him a heart that is focused on integrity and righteousness. Help him to be a man of his word and to lead his life with honesty and sincerity. I pray he be a shining example of your love and grace to all those around him, and may his actions and words reflect the goodness of your character. Help him to be a good steward of his responsibilities and to conduct the affairs of our home with a heart that is pure and blameless. I thank you, Lord, that his heart is being purified every day. Help me to nurture it as his help meet.

In the name of Jesus, I pray, Amen.

February 8

"Make a joyful shout to the Lord, all you lands!"
(Psalm 100: 1a)

Dear Lord, today I make a joyful noise to you! Hallelujah! You are great and greatly to be praised. You are
worthy of all the praise! You are the King of kings and
the Lord of lords. There is none like you! I praise you
today and I thank you Father for a husband that
praises you as well. I praise you and thank you that his
life and speech will always honor you. I pray that you
would fill him with zeal to bless your name! Let him
catch a divine revelation of who you are, so that he
may shout unashamed and tell others about your
greatness!

In the name of Jesus, I pray, Amen.

February 9

*"Serve the Lord with gladness; Come before His presence with singing." (**Psalm 100:2**)*

Dear Lord, what a privilege it is to serve you! You make our hearts glad. Today I pray that my husband may always remember the goodness and faithfulness of your character, and I pray he offers you his heartfelt gratitude for all the blessings in his life. Help him to see the beauty of your creation and the wonder of your love, and I pray he worships you with all his heart, soul, mind, and strength. Lord, I pray that his worship would be a sweet aroma to you and that it would bring him closer to your presence. I pray he experiences the joy of your salvation and the peace that surpasses all understanding. I pray that we continue to worship together and come before Your presence with singing. As we worship together Lord, we are unified in Your Name. Cancel the plans of the enemy that come to divide us.

In the name of Jesus, I pray, Amen.

59

February 10

"He who is slow to wrath has great understanding, But he who is impulsive exalts folly." **(Proverbs 14:29)**

Dear Lord, I thank you for a husband who possesses great understanding. I praise you for a man of patience. As he draws closer to you, I pray that you would increase his understanding. I declare and decree that wrath has no place in our home or in our marriage. We are both slow to speak and quick to listen. We will edify one another with our speech and display the fruit of the spirit in our lives. Teach us how to communicate with one another with grace and love.

In the name of Jesus, I pray, Amen.

February *11*

"Get wisdom! Get understanding! Do not forget, nor turn away from the words of my mouth. Do not forsake her, and she will preserve you; Love her, and she will keep you. Wisdom is the principal thing; Therefore get wisdom. And in all your getting, get understanding."
(Proverbs 4:5 – 7)

Dear Lord, I come before you today on behalf of my beloved husband, and I pray that he will seek wisdom and understanding. Lord, I ask that you give him a hunger for your truth and a thirst for knowledge that can only be found in you. Help him to seek after you with all his heart, and I pray he finds the wisdom and understanding he needs to navigate the challenges of life as well as the challenges in our marriage. Give him discernment and insight as he makes decisions, and I pray he always chooses the path that leads to righteousness. Thank you for your promise to give your wisdom liberally to anyone who asks.

In the name of Jesus, I pray, Amen.

February 12

*"May the Lord cause you to flourish, both you and your children." (**Proverbs 115:14**)*

Dear Lord, I lift my husband to you today and ask for your abundant blessings to be upon him. I pray that you would fill his heart with your love, joy, and peace. I pray that he would experience your goodness and faithfulness in all areas of his life. May his work and his relationships be fruitful, and I pray he be a source of inspiration and encouragement to those around him. Lord, bless our children as well and help us to be good parents who guide them in your ways. May our family be a testimony to your grace and love and may we all flourish and grow in your presence. Thank you for your mercy and provision, and we trust in you for all our needs.

In the name of Jesus, I pray, Amen.

February *13*

"Holy Father, protect them by the power of your name, the name you gave me, so that they may be one as we are one." (John 17: 11b)

Dear Lord, I come before you today with a heart full of gratitude for my husband. I pray the same prayer that Jesus prayed, therefore I know that it is already done. I pray for my husband's protection and that you will keep him safe from the evil one and protect him from harm, by the power of Your Name. Help him to live a life that brings honor and glory to your name and give him the strength to persevere through any trials or challenges that he may face today. Thank you for the gift of my husband, and I pray that you will continue to bless him and guide him in all his ways.

In the name of Jesus, I pray, Amen.

February *14*

*"So that Christ may dwell in your hearts through faith.
And I pray that you, being rooted and established in love,
may have power, together with all the Lord's holy people,
to grasp how wide and long and high and deep is the love
of Christ, and to know this love that surpasses knowledge—that you may be filled to the measure of all the
fullness of God." **(Ephesians 3:17-19)***

Dear Lord, today I pray that my husband would make
his heart a dwelling place for you, through faith. I pray
that he is rooted and that his foundation is love. With
all that he has been through, disappointments, and
hurts, give him the holy insight to fully grasp the
depth of your love for him. Show him that your love is
unfailing. Miraculously show that love to him today. I
pray that you would continuously fill him with more of
you and that his prayer is simply to desire more of
you.

In the name of Jesus, I pray, Amen.

February 15

"Now to him who is able to do immeasurably more than all we ask or imagine, according to his power that is at work within us," **(Ephesians 3:20)**

Dear Lord, today I pray for my beloved husband that you will bless him abundantly according to your power that is at work within him. Help him to trust in your plans and purposes for his life and give him the strength and courage to pursue them with all his heart. Fill him with your wisdom, and discernment, and guide him in all his decisions. I pray he knows that he is loved and cherished by you. I pray he experiences your presence and peace today. Thank you for being the God who can do infinitely more than we can ask or imagine.

In the name of Jesus, I pray, Amen.

February 16

"But as for me, it is good to be near God."
(Psalm 73:28a)

Dear Lord, thank you for your nearness. Thank you that your word says you will never leave or forsake us. I pray for a husband who understands that truth and has made you his resting place. I pray that my husband begins to grasp the depth of goodness that comes with being close to you. Thank you, Lord, for a husband who has made you his first defense. Lord, I pray for him to develop a longing within to be near you. May his affections toward you be pure and authentic, causing him to fall in love with you over and over.

In the name of Jesus, I pray, Amen.

February 17

"I have made the Sovereign Lord my refuge; I will tell of all your deeds." (Psalm 73:28b)

Dear Lord, I thank you for being our refuge. In this world with so many distractions, there is the temptation to take refuge in many things. I pray that my husband comes to you for safety and acceptance. Make him know his identity in you. Thank you that he does not look to the world for his needs. Help him find his way and remind him that he can take refuge in you. Dear Lord, whenever the time calls, help me to be attentive to his needs and always respond in a way that leads him back to you. Thank you that he brings glory to you by telling others of your good works.

In the name of Jesus, I pray, Amen.

February 18

"'And it shall be in the last days,' God says, 'That I will pour out My Spirit on all mankind; And your sons and your daughters will prophesy, And your young men will see visions, And your old men will have dreams;"
(Acts 2: 17)

Dear Lord, we are living in the final days. Thank you for pouring out Your Spirit on all humanity, including my husband, myself, and our children. I pray that you would give him visions and as he grows old you would speak to him in his dreams. Give him the ability to see things through your eyes. I ask for a fresh outpouring of Your Spirit on my husband and everything connected to him. Speak to him in dreams and visions. Enlighten, empower, and direct. Dear Lord, soften his heart, to hear your voice and to follow your leading.

In the name of Jesus, I pray, Amen.

February 19

"Don't let anyone look down on you because you are young, but set an example for the believers in speech, in conduct, in love, in faith and in purity."
(1 Timothy 4:12)

Dear Lord, thank you for the access we have to, and through you! Thank you for my husband's walk and his talk. Thank you that he can approach your throne boldly and walk around with blessed assurance because he is yours. Holy Spirit, please remind him of that truth. I thank you Lord that my husband is an example to other believers in the way he talks, walks, loves, and how he shows his faith in God. I thank you that he is being made pure in you. Thank you that this fruit is not for show, but that he is the example of great faith in our home first.

In the name of Jesus, I pray, Amen.

February 20

"He put a new song in my mouth, a hymn of praise to our God." (Psalm 40:3a)

Dear Lord, I praise you for who you are. Thank you for making me aware of the importance of praying for my husband. I may not know everything that he is going through today, but I pray that you would fill my husband with more of you. Put a new song in his mouth. Give him a new perspective. If he has been meditating on the bad, I pray that you would shift his focus. Let the words of his mouth be acceptable in your sight. Let him not be a complainer, but one who chooses to praise, offering new songs and a hymn of praise to you!

In the name of Jesus, I pray, Amen.

February 21

*"May the God of hope fill you with all joy and peace as you trust in him, so that you may overflow with hope by the power of the Holy Spirit." (**Romans 15:13**)*

Dear Lord, I praise and thank you for my husband. In his life, I am aware that there have been many instances that have caused him not to trust fully. Mend his heart so that he is open to truly trusting again. God of hope, fill my husband with unending hope. And as he trusts more and more in you, fill him with joy and supernatural peace, so that hope overflows out of him. Let it be contagious, Lord. Holy Spirit, do a mighty work!

In the name of Jesus, I pray, Amen.

February 22

"You have made known to me the ways of life; You will fill me [infusing my soul] with joy with Your presence."
(Acts 2:28)

Dear Lord, I pray in advance and thank you for making known the ways of life to my husband. Thank you for infusing his soul with joy because you are near. Help him to sense your presence when things are loud. Help him to sense your presence when he feels alone. Help him to sense your presence when he needs guidance. Because, in your presence, we find everything we need. Give him wisdom on how to navigate through life. Let him lean not on his understanding but direct him to lean on the word for instruction in his life. You are so good, and your mercy endures forever. Thank you for being a merciful God.

In the name of Jesus, I pray, Amen.

February 23

"Fools mock sin [but sin mocks the fools], But among the upright there is good will and the favor and blessing of God." **(Proverbs 14:9)**

Dear Lord, I thank you for placing your mighty hand on and over my husband. I thank you, Lord, that my husband walks uprightly and does good to others. Dismantle past teachings and examples he may have heard that minimized the seriousness of sin and its consequences. I pray he takes heed of the weight of sin, all while seeking righteousness for Your Name's sake. Thank you for the favor and blessing of God that rests on his life all because he walks uprightly before you, Lord. Get the glory out of his life.

In the name of Jesus, I pray, Amen.

February 24

"Many will see and fear the Lord and put their trust in him." (Psalm 40:3b)

Dear Lord, thank you for the miracles, signs, and wonders you have performed in my husband's life. Thank you, Lord, that he is one of the "Many" that see and fear you. Lord, I pray he acquires a genuine reverence for you. Your word says the fear of the Lord is the beginning of wisdom. I pray that my husband has that fear and that it becomes more and more evident in his life. I pray he trusts in you with all his heart and lean not on his understanding, but in all his ways acknowledge you so that you can direct his path. Thank you that he is learning every day to trust in You and only You.

In the name of Jesus, I pray, Amen.

February 25

"For I have chosen him, so that he will direct his children and his household after him to keep the way of the Lord by doing what is right and just, so that the Lord will bring about for Abraham what he has promised him."
(Genesis 18:19)

Dear Lord, your word says many are called, but few are chosen. Thank you for choosing my husband. Thank you that he has a purpose in you. I thank you, Lord, for a man of God that directs our children and our household in your way. Thank you that he delights in doing what is right and fair and that he is and is becoming the father and husband you created him to be. Thank you that he has taken a stand against generational sin and that he works hard to walk uprightly, modeling the way of the Lord before us. I praise you for my husband.

In the name of Jesus, I pray, Amen.

February 26

*"The Lord is my shepherd, I lack nothing." **(Psalm 23:1)***

Dear Lord, thank you. Thank you for giving us everything we need. We lack nothing. Thank you, Lord, that my husband realizes that because he has you, he lacks nothing. This means that everything he needs; physically, emotionally, mentally, spiritually, and financially, he can find in you. He does not have to lack. Enlarge his territories, Lord. Increase his confidence in you. Be everything that he needs to feel complete and competent in you.

In the name of Jesus, I pray, Amen.

February 27

"He makes me lie down in green pastures, he leads me beside quiet waters," **(Psalm 23:2)**

Dear Lord, thank you for a husband that embraces rest. Give him the wisdom to know when he needs to rest. The beautiful thing about green pastures is that they are beautiful and bountiful. Show him the beauty and benefits that come with resting in you. Lead him, direct his heart, and calm his spirit. Quiet the noise in his life. Eliminate distractions. Speak to him, like only you can, to guide him when he needs to rest and retreat. Show him that rest is a wise act and not a sign of weakness.

In the name of Jesus, I pray, Amen.

February 28

"He refreshes my soul. He guides me along the right paths for his name's sake." (Psalm 23:3)

Dear Lord, thank you for being a refreshing God. With the weight of the world that my husband carries with work, family, and his silent personal battles, I pray that a supernatural refreshing will come upon him, in the name of Jesus. Wherever he is today, let him be overwhelmed by your presence and the refreshing of the Holy Spirit. Take his hand, Lord, and guide him along the right paths; not only for his good, but for Your Name's sake. Order his steps. For you said that the Lord orders the steps of a good man. I thank you for a good man, Lord! I thank you.

In the name of Jesus, I pray, Amen.

February 29

*"Even though I walk through the darkest valley, I will fear no evil, for you are with me; your rod and your staff, they comfort me." **(Psalm 23:4)***

Dear Lord, thank you for never leaving or forsaking us! Thank you for being with my husband through his darkest valley. Thank you for the confidence that we have in you because your word proclaims that you are with us. And Lord, if he has not reached his darkest valley yet, when he does, because of life's blows, show him that you are always there. Let Your Presence be felt in his lowest moments. Comfort him when he is sad or confused. Make Your Presence known in his life. Overwhelm my husband with your reckless love for him.

In the name of Jesus, I pray, Amen.

MARCH

March 1

"Therefore, if anyone is in Christ, he is a new creation; old things have passed away; behold, all things have become new." (2 Corinthians 5:17)

Dear Lord, I thank you that my husband is developing into the man you have called him to be. Help him to realize that he can let go of his old self and embrace the new. Reveal to him the awesomeness that comes with being an actual new being, in you! Give him Holy Ghost confidence when he doubts himself. Lord, I pray that you would, gently take his hand and show him how to embrace the new creation you have made him. Give him the desire and the courage to let go of the past. Break the strongholds in his mind that are keeping him bound and causing him to believe that he is incapable of being a new creation, in the Name of Jesus! Thank you for a new husband! Thank you for the revelation of You and the newness that comes with "being in You!"

In the name of Jesus, I pray, Amen.

March 2

*"In peace I will lie down and sleep, for you alone, Lord make me dwell in safety." **(Psalm 4:8)***

Dear Lord, thank you for your peace that surpasses all our understanding. Give my husband that peace. When he lies down to sleep, rid his mind of the troubles of the day and the weight that he carries. Remind him that he can cast all his cares on you because you care. Block the plans of the enemy that have been orchestrated to interrupt his rest, in the name of Jesus. Grant him sweet rest and impart divine revelation that will lead him on the path to righteousness.

In the name of Jesus, I pray, Amen.

March 3

*"I will strengthen you: I will help you: I will uphold you
with the right hand of my righteousness."*
(Isaiah 41:10)

Dear Lord, your word says you will strengthen, help,
and uphold us with the right hand of your righteousness. I pray that you would do just that right now
for my husband; especially today. Strengthen him
where he is weak, help him where he is afraid to ask
for help, and uphold him with your right hand. Give
him the courage to do what is right when all signs
around him are pointing in the wrong direction. And
Lord, if there is any fear in my husband, I bind that
spirit by the authority of Jesus Christ and command it
to leave his presence. Make my husband know that he
does not have to be afraid because you are near.
Strengthen him Lord, and I pray he feels your help as
you uphold him with your mighty right hand. Give
him godly confidence that he can conquer anything
with you by his side.

In the name of Jesus, I pray, Amen.

March 4

"Do not be wise in your own eyes; Fear the Lord and depart from evil." **(Proverbs 3:7)**

Dear Lord, thank you for the wisdom of the Lord that is given to anyone who asks of you. I pray for my husband today and declare that if there is deception in his life that has led him to believe that he is wise in his own eyes, I renounce and take authority over it, in the name of Jesus. By the Power and Authority of Jesus Christ, I bind the spirit of deception and command it to leave my husband's presence, his mind, and his being. Give him the eyes of Christ so that he can see and detect evil, even when it is cloaked in sheep's clothing. Give him the wisdom to flee.

In the name of Jesus, I pray, Amen.

March 5

*"Then the way you live will always honor and please the Lord, and your lives will produce every kind of good fruit. All the while, you will grow as you learn to know God better and better." **(Colossians 9:10)***

Dear Lord, I thank you for blessing me and our family with a man that always honors and pleases you with his lifestyle. May the fruit he produces be good and glorify you, Father. I thank you that his life produces every kind of good fruit - love, joy, peace, patience, kindness, goodness, gentleness, faithfulness, and self-control. Lord, I thank you for leading my husband by Your Spirit and allowing the fruit of the Spirit to flow to and through him. I pray that you would plant our family in a word-based church where we are growing and learning more and more about you each day.

In the name of Jesus, I pray, Amen.

March 6

*"Sing a new song to the Lord! Let the whole earth sing to the Lord!" **(Psalm 96:1)***

Dear Lord, let me join in with the whole earth and sing praises to you today! You are amazing! Thank you, Lord, for giving my husband a new song and that praise is on his lips. I pray he joins in with other worshippers and sing songs to you. Give him the wisdom to know that in times of distress, he can lift his praises to magnify you and not the present circumstance. I pray for boldness to sing a new song to you. You are so deserving, Lord!

In the name of Jesus, I pray, Amen.

March 7

*"Sing to the Lord; praise his name. Each day proclaim the good news that he saves." **(Psalm 96:2)***

Dear Lord, I praise your name today because you are good, and your mercy endures forever! Thank you, Lord! Thank you that you ARE the good news and that you sent Jesus to save us! Today I praise you for my husband and pray for his mind and his speech. Thank you, Lord, that his words are wholesome and life-giving. I thank you that each day he chooses to tell others about the good news of Jesus Christ and how you have made a difference in his life. Lord, thank you that his life is a testament to your goodness and love!

In the name of Jesus, I pray, Amen.

March 8

"Your word is a lamp for my feet, a light on my path."
(Psalm 119:105)

Dear Lord, thank you for being the lamp to my husband's feet and the light on his path. Lead him on the path of righteousness for Your Name's sake and show him where to go when he is stuck at a crossroad. Give him holy resolve to trust you in the valley of decision and to take steps with confidence knowing you are guiding him and that you have his back. Lord, thank you for a husband that delights in the word and uses it to lead and guide him. Thank you that your word is hidden in his heart and that he is a man that does not operate outside of it.

In the name of Jesus, I pray, Amen.

March 9

*"My son, do not despise the chastening of the Lord, nor detest His correction." (**Proverbs 3:11**)*

Dear Lord, I thank you for a husband that loves you so much that he has made you priority in his life. Even though it may be hard, I pray that he sees your correction as love and that he does not despise your chastening. Thank you, Lord, that he understands that if you are correcting him, it is because you love Him, and it is good for him. It is the goodness of the Lord that leads to repentance. Thank you that he is not a prideful man, but full of humility and mature enough to receive your rebuke. I pray he walks in the light of your salvation.

In the name of Jesus, I pray, Amen.

March 10

*"So we have not stopped praying for you since we first heard about you. We ask God to give you complete knowledge of his will and to give you spiritual wisdom and understanding." **(Colossians 1:9)***

Dear Lord, just as Paul prayed, I pray also for my husband. I will not stop praying for him nor will I cease giving thanks to you in advance for giving my husband complete knowledge of your will. I pray that you would give him insight into his purpose and that you would please grant him spiritual wisdom and understanding. I pray he grasp the depth of your wisdom and apply it in every area of his life.

In the name of Jesus, I pray, Amen.

March 11

"Righteousness guards the person of integrity, but wickedness overthrows the sinner." (Proverbs 13:6)

Dear Lord, I thank you for my husband who is a man of honor. I pray that you would give him the strength to walk with integrity as he makes decisions today. Let his light shine before men so that ultimately you get the glory! Thank you that righteousness guards him. I thank you for a husband who is a good decision-maker that takes into consideration the consequences of his choices. I praise you that he is not overthrown by wickedness but motivated by righteousness. Thank you for rescuing his life! Lord, bless his life today in a new and fresh way.

In the name of Jesus, I pray, Amen.

March 12

"The wages of the righteous is life, but the earnings of the wicked are sin and death." ***(Proverbs 10: 16)***

Dear Lord, I praise you for the wonderful exchange that comes with serving you! Your word declares the wages of sin is death but the gift to the righteous is life. I pray for my husband today and ask that you would give him life abundantly. I pray he recognizes the favor of God that comes with serving you. Thank you for forgiving our sins and giving us an abundant life. Thank you that he earns life because of his righteous living. Expand every area of his life. Thank you, Lord, for a holy and righteous man.

In the name of Jesus, I pray, Amen.

March 13

"Blessed are those who hunger and thirst for right-eousness, for they will be filled." **(Matthew 5:6)**

Dear Lord, I come to you in deep gratitude for my husband today. I pray that whatever state of mind he is in today, you would fill my husband with love, joy, and peace. Thank you that he hungers and thirsts for what is right. Thank you that he finds fulfillment in you and that he does not turn to the things of the world for validation and confidence. Turn his face and focus on you when the way of the world seeks to over-take him. Cover him with your blood. Fill him with more of you and continue to develop a hunger and thirst for you. Even now, Lord, I pray that you would fill his empty spaces with more of you.

In the name of Jesus, I pray, Amen.

March 14

"Jesus answered, "It is written: 'Man shall not live on bread alone, but on every word that comes from the mouth of God." (Matthew 4:4)

Dear Lord, I pray for a husband that loves the Word. That means he loves you! Thank you, Lord, that my husband seeks first the kingdom and all your righteousness. I pray right now that where he has made his belly (appetites) his god, you would reveal it to him. Develop in him a desire where he thrives from every word that comes from your mouth. I thank you for a man that is awake spiritually and when the enemy comes to tempt him, knows how to use the Word as his weapon of defense. Strengthen his spiritual muscles today, Lord.

In the name of Jesus, I pray, Amen.

March 15

"For David says of Him, 'I saw the Lord continually be-fore me, Because He is at my right hand, so that I will not be shaken." (Acts 2:25)

Dear Lord, wherever he is and whatever he is doing today, be at his right hand. I pray that you would cover my husband under your mighty wings. May my husband continually see only you before him. When the enemy comes in like a flood and he begins to get discouraged, remind him that you are at his right hand, and he will not be shaken. You are faithful. You are a loving God. Build up his confidence in you. Eliminate and annihilate the distractions in his life today. Make him see, with spiritual vision, the traps the enemy has set to make him fall. Give him the spiritual stamina to stand against the wiles of the enemy.

In the name of Jesus, I pray, Amen.

March 16

"You are the light of the world. A city on a hill cannot be hidden." (Matthew 5:14a)

Dear Lord, I praise you because my husband is fearfully and wonderfully made. What a mighty man you have created for your glory! Thank you for choosing him to represent you. Thank you, Lord, for a man of God that is not ashamed to be a disciple of Christ. Thank you that he shines his light wherever he goes. I thank you for a man who radiates your love. May his light be contagious and those around him see You in him. When he is positioned on a hill professionally, in ministry, with friends, and even with family, give him the capacity to handle the pressure and represent you like a champion!

In the name of Jesus, I pray, Amen.

March 17

"If you are insulted and reviled for [bearing] the name of Christ, you are blessed [happy, with life-joy and comfort in God's salvation regardless of your circumstances], because the Spirit of glory and of God is resting on you [and indwelling you—He whom they curse, you glorify]."
(1 Peter 4:14)

Dear Lord, I thank you that the Spirit of glory and Your Spirit rests on my husband. Bless his life, Lord. Fill him with the joy and comfort that comes with your saving grace. Whatever circumstance he faces today, remind him of the joy you have already blessed him with that is accessible in your presence. Thank you for a man of God who is honored to serve you. Thank you that when he is insulted, ridiculed, or even discriminated against because of you, he feels blessed. Thank you that the Spirit of glory and your Spirit rest on him. Grant him sweet rest in his soul, mind, will, and emotions.

In the name of Jesus, I pray, Amen.

March 18

"Showing yourself to be an example of good works in every way. In your teaching show integrity, dignity,"
(Titus 2:7)

Dear Lord, I praise you for your goodness. Your word declares that a good man brings forth good things out of the goodness of his heart. I thank you that my husband shows himself to be an example of your good work in every area of his life. Thank you that he is a good steward of the things you have blessed him with. Thank you that he is my good thing, and you continue to make him a good husband. Thank you that he is a good father. Thank you that his lifestyle teaches goodness and that he continues to show integrity and dignity consistently. When he wants to give up, arise in him to remind him who he is in You.

In the name of Jesus, I pray, Amen.

March 19

"For this is the way God loved the world: He gave his one and only Son, so that everyone who believes in him will not perish but have eternal life." (John 3:16)

Dear Lord, thank you for loving us so much! I praise you for sending your only son to pay the debt for sin. Thank you, Lord, for not only paying the debt but for also conquering death on the cross, which makes us victorious in every area of our lives. Because of the gift of Jesus Christ, my husband has eternal life. Lord, if my husband has not yet come to know you as his Lord and Savior, I pray that you would make yourself known in his life. If he has wandered, draw him back to you. I praise and thank you in advance that he is a citizen in the kingdom of God, and he walks daily in his inheritance of eternal life.

In the name of Jesus, I pray, Amen.

March 20

"let the one who believes in me drink. Just as the scripture says, 'From within him will flow rivers of living water."
(John 7:38)

Dear Lord, thank you for being our living well who never runs dry. Although this world may offer many things to drink, today I thank you Lord that my husband drinks from the living well. I am so grateful that you have created a man with great conviction and strength. Because he believes in you, he drinks (partakes in) what is right, and from within him flows rivers of living water. May these rivers of living water empower him to live out his purpose while being a blessing to the world around him.

In the name of Jesus, I pray, Amen.

March 21

"But Peter and the apostles answered and said, We must obey God rather than men." (Acts 5:29)

Dear Lord, I thank you that my husband has a firm foundation in you. I pray that he continues to see you. Deepen his desire to know you. Give him the conviction to stand against the status quo and to demonstrate obedience to you rather than to man. Strengthen him with your resurrection power to conquer the challenges he may be facing today. I thank you for surrounding him, increasing in him, and giving him the boldness, he needs to conquer anything. Give him unshakable peace as he continues to obey you.

In the name of Jesus, I pray, Amen.

March 22

"I have told you these things so that in me you may have peace. In the world you have trouble and suffering, but take courage—I have conquered the world."
(John 16:33)

Dear Lord, thank you for sacrificing your life and for overcoming the world. You endured the cross for our peace. Today I pray that my husband would tap into that peace. Give him the mindset to seek you for his peace and not to seek after other things or other people; not even me. You are his peace. Remind him during those challenging times that you have won the victory. Therefore, he is more than a conqueror. The enemy has been defeated. He does fight for victory but fights from victory. Lord, show him how to take courage and find rest in you.

In the name of Jesus, I pray, Amen.

March 23

"He gives strength to those who are tired; to the ones who lack power, he gives renewed energy." **(Isaiah 40:29)**

Dear Lord, I praise you because everything we need is in you. Thank you, Lord, for giving my husband renewed strength from day to day. I pray that where his power is lacking, you would refresh, refill, and renew his energy. Release your heavenly strength even now, Lord. I pray he feels you in his bones, in his muscles, in his mind and his spirit. Thank you that he is a husband that takes delight in working to take care of his family. Renew his strength, Lord. When he pours out, refill him. Thank you for such a mighty man of valor.

In the name of Jesus, I pray, Amen.

March 24

"For freedom, Christ has set us free. Stand firm, then, and do not be subject again to the yoke of slavery."
(Galatians 5:1)

Dear Lord, I thank you that we are free in you! What a gift! Today I pray for my husband's understanding of the freedom that he has in you. I pray that you would reveal to him areas of bondage where the enemy has deceived him. Free him from shame connected to past decisions, trauma, and circumstances in his life that have kept him bound. Remind him that he is no longer a slave to his past and past sins, but that he is free because you set us free! Give him the confidence to stand firm in his deliverance. Fill him with a holy confidence to conquer his weaknesses and to not be subject again to the yoke of slavery.

In the name of Jesus, I pray, Amen.

March 25

"Be ye therefore, imitators of God, as beloved children,"
(Ephesians 5:1)

Dear Lord, thank you for calling us your children. Thank you that you are our inheritance. You are a good, good father. Father, although my husband may not have had the best examples, I am grateful for your example in his life. Thank you for giving him the confidence to be an imitator of God. I bind any spirit of fear of failure, in the name of Jesus, that may be present to make him feel defeated or unworthy to be called a son of God. Thank you for your example of unconditional love. Give my husband the capacity and desire to love me, our family, and others like you have first loved him.

In the name of Jesus, I pray, Amen.

March 26

"I thank my God every time I remember you. I always pray with joy in my every prayer for all of you."
(Philippians 1:3-4)

Dear Lord, I just want to take this moment, not to ask for anything, but to simply thank you for my husband. Thank you for bringing us together. Thank you for being God in his life. Thank you for my anointed, amazing, and loving husband! That is my prayer today! A prayer of thanksgiving. Thank you, Lord, for my husband!

In the name of Jesus, I pray, Amen.

(And if you do not know who he is yet, consider this a prayer of faith, believing God for what is to come!!!)

March 27

"For I am sure of this very thing, that the one who began a good work in you will perfect it until the day of Christ Jesus." (Philippians 1:6)

Dear Lord, you are amazing! You are the Creator of all. I praise you for creating my husband and for the "good work" you have started within him. I thank you that you are not finished with my husband yet. Thank you for the truth of your Word which declares that what you have begun in him, you will perfect it, maturing him until the day of your return. Perfect in him the gifts, desires, and purpose you have placed in him.

I thank you for a mature man of God who listens to your Word and moves in obedience. Continue to cultivate in him that which You have placed in him to show forth Your glory.

In the name of Jesus, I pray, Amen.

March 28

"Let your speech always be gracious, seasoned with salt,
so that you may know how you should answer everyone."
(Colossians 4:6)

Dear Lord, you are the perfect example of gracious
speech. Thank you for a husband that speaks with
grace and wisdom. I praise you for a husband that is
quick to listen and slow to speak. I thank you, Lord,
that he walks the walk and talks the talk. I praise you
that my husband is about your business. I pray he has
gracious speech in our home, with me and our children; seasoned with salt to bring flavor and be the
perfect ingredient. Thank you that his speech is seasoned with truth and clarity and that he communi-
cates with everyone with such grace and truth.

In the name of Jesus, I pray, Amen.

March 29

"And may the Lord cause you to increase and abound in love for one another and for all, just as we do for you,"
(1 Thessalonians 3:12)

Dear Lord, your word says that there is no greater love than this; that a man would lay down his life for a friend. Thank you for laying down your life and becoming love in the flesh. I pray for my husband today and ask that you would fill him with your love. Your love is patient. Your love is kind. It does not envy or boast. It is not arrogant or rude. It does not insist on its own way. It is not irritable or resentful. Nor does it rejoice in wrongdoing. But it rejoices with the truth and never fails. Dear Jesus, fill my husband with that type of love. Cause him to increase and abound in that type of love for others. For you, God, are love. Teach him to love as you do.

In the name of Jesus, I pray, Amen.

March 30

"so that your hearts are strengthened in holiness to be blameless before our God and Father at the coming of our Lord Jesus with all his saints." (1 Thessalonians 3:13)

Dear Lord, as you continue to teach my husband how to love, I pray that you would strengthen his heart in holiness so that he may be blameless before you when you return. I pray for a husband that is dedicated and consecrated to you. I thank you for leading my husband. Let holiness and Your righteousness lead him in all that he does. Give him confidence in knowing that he can walk holy and upright before you and man. Let him know that it is possible to be blameless before you. Encourage his heart, mind, and soul.

In the name of Jesus, I pray, Amen.

March 31

"But you, dear friends, by building yourselves up in your most holy faith, by praying in the Holy Spirit, maintain yourselves in the love of God, while anticipating the mercy of our Lord Jesus Christ that brings eternal life."
(Jude 1:20-21)

Dear Lord, I pray that you would continue to build up my husband in his most holy faith. Strengthen his faith. Remind my husband to pray in the Holy Spirit to build himself up in his most holy faith; and if he does not know how, bring enlightenment to his life. Place him around the right body of Christ that can nurture his faith and teach him how to grow in you. Lord, show him the way or lead him to the right example(s) to show him how. Close doors that no man can open and open doors that no man can close. Saturate him in Your love. Let him feel Your mercy, let him abide in Your Love. Bring awareness to the mercy that surrounds him, which brings eternal life.

In the name of Jesus, I pray, Amen.

365 PRAYERS FOR YOUR HUSBAND

APRIL

April 1

"Dear friend, I pray that all may go well with you and that you may be in good health, just as it is well with your soul." (3 John 1:2)

Dear Lord, today I pray for my husband's health. I plead the Blood of Jesus over his mind, body, and soul. Your word says that you heal all diseases. Lord, I pray that you will keep him from physical sickness and mental disease. I bind the spirit of infirmity in the name of Jesus, and I command his health to line up with Your Word, which declares, "By Your stripes, he is healed." I pray that all may go well with my husband and thank you in advance for his good health, just as it is well with his soul. Make him more conscious and aware of the choices that affect his health. Lead him on a journey to wellness.

In the name of Jesus, I pray, Amen.

April 2

"We demolish arguments and every pretension that sets itself up against the knowledge of God, and we take captive every thought to make it obedient to Christ."
(2 Corinthians 10:5)

Dear Lord Jesus, thank you for my husband's healing. Adding to yesterday's prayer, and according to your word, I demolish every stronghold, argument, and pretentious thought that sets itself up against the knowledge of God, in the mighty Name of Jesus. I know that you are great and mighty. I know that you do all things well. I know that everything we need is in you. I know that you will never leave us or forsake us. With the authority of Jesus Christ, I take captive every mind-binding thought, lie, or stronghold that has deceived my husband and kept him bound and command it to come into obedience to Christ!

In the name of Jesus, I pray, Amen.

April 3

*"So get rid of all evil and all deceit and hypocrisy and envy and all slander." (**1 Peter 2:1**)*

Dear Lord, today I thank you for your presence being known in my husband's life. Go before him to reveal and get rid of all evil, deceit, hypocrisy, envy, and slander. In the mighty Name of Jesus, I bind the enemy that tries to invade our marriage, our home, our places of work, or any other area in our lives. I declare and decree that our home is a safe place filled with love, truth, goodness, kindness, and joy. Father, let your holy presence continue to fill our hearts and the spaces we occupy.

In the name of Jesus, I pray, Amen.

April 4

"But if you fulfill the royal law as expressed in this scripture, 'You shall love your neighbor as yourself,' you are doing well." ***(James 2:8)***

Dear Lord, I pray that you teach my husband and me to love one another with unconditional love. Heal the wounds of his broken heart so that he can expect and experience real love. Prepare our minds to receive love from one another and our bodies to express our affections. Thank you for the desire and the wisdom to love one another well. Show him how to love others like You and create divine opportunities to demonstrate that love. I decree and declare that my husband will minister the love of Christ.

In the name of Jesus, I pray, Amen.

April 5

"Now faith is being sure of what we hope for, being convinced of what we do not see." (Hebrews 11:1)

Dear Lord, give my husband a deeper revelation of you and strengthen his faith daily. I pray he has the confidence to trust you for what he does not see and the boldness to be sure of what he has seen. Allow my faith to be his anchor and a reminder that God cannot and will not ever fail. Therefore, any past failures, disappointments, and distractions that may have caused him to waiver in his faith will no longer capture his focus. From this day forward, my husband will demonstrate a faith that testifies of your power and ability to do all things.

In the name of Jesus, I pray, Amen.

April 6

"I pray that the faith you share with us may deepen your understanding of every blessing that belongs to you in Christ." (Philemon 1:6)

Dear Lord, thank you for a husband who recognizes all that belongs to him belongs to You. I pray that you will continue to bless the works of his hands all for your glory. Lord, reveal to him the significance of every blessing, restore all that is rightfully his, and lead him to recover what belongs to him. You have blessed the life of my husband so abundantly and I pray that he reciprocates those blessings to others.

In the name of Jesus, I pray, Amen.

April 7

*"Where there is strife, there is pride, but wisdom is found in those who take advice." (**Proverbs 13:10**)*

Dear Lord, thank you for a wise husband. I am grateful for a husband that is not prideful. He is a man of grace, humility, and peace. Therefore, our marriage is full of grace, humility, and peace. I pray for our marriage today, that my husband and our marriage reflect Your character. I pray that my husband will continue to seek wisdom and advice from wise counsel.

In the name of Jesus, I pray, Amen.

April 8

"We also pray that you will be strengthened with all the glorious power so you will have all the endurance and patience you need." (Colossians 9:11)

Dear Lord, today I pray for my husband's strength to be revealed and increased within him. You are the source of his strength. Supply him with all that he needs. Lord, I thank you for a husband who is strong in mind, body, and soul. You are mighty. Therefore, he is mighty because of you. Remind him that the same power that raised Jesus from the dead lives within him. I pray for him to have endurance and patience today and every day.

In the name of Jesus, I pray, Amen.

April 9

"When a man's ways please the Lord, He makes even his enemies to be at peace with him." **(Proverbs 16:7)**

Dear Lord, thank you for being my husband's defender and protector. You are faithful and such a good Father to him. Thank you Lord that my husband's desire is to live for and to please you. I thank you for a husband that lives with the utmost integrity, especially when no one is looking. I pray that his ways please you, Lord. AND if they don't, speak to his heart. Where there may be hardness of heart, only you can mend it. Mend his heart, Jesus. Let his ways please you so that you can make his enemies be at peace with him. Thank you for that promise.

In the name of Jesus, I pray, Amen.

April 10

*"But whosoever drinketh of the water that I shall give him shall never thirst, but the water that I shall give him shall be in him a well of water springing up into everlasting life." (**John 4:14**)*

Dear Lord, because we drink the water you give, we will never thirst again. You are a well of water that is springing up into everlasting life. I am thankful for a husband who seeks to quench his thirst in you and not give into the desires of his flesh. He knows that nothing else will satisfy him as you can. Lead him to the place overflowing with your water and your Spirit.

In the name of Jesus, I pray, Amen.

April 11

"Turn away from evil. Do what is right. Then you will en-joy lasting security." (Psalm 37:27)

Dear Lord, thank you for my husband who does not take any delight in evil. He shuns the appearance of evil and swiftly turns from it. He is a man of God, endeavoring to always do what is right even when it is not popular or comfortable. Thank you for the lasting security he has in you and for the peace he experiences because he willfully seeks to do what is right. When the days seem hard, whisper in his ear reminding him that you are as near as the mention of Your name.

In the name of Jesus, I pray, Amen.

April 12

"Iron sharpens iron; so a man sharpeneth the countenance of his friend." **(Proverbs 27:17)**

Dear Lord, I thank you for the gift of fellowship and friendship with my husband. Bless our time together. Let our shared love for you, your Word, and for one another lead us to the sharpening of each other's countenance. I pray for the immediate removal of negative influences. Lord, replace them with Holy Spirit-filled friends and brothers that will equip him to be the man you created for a purpose; men that will enrich his life with wisdom, and those who will encourage him to live by faith.

In the name of Jesus, I pray, Amen.

April 13

*"Every word of God is purified; he is like a shield for those who take refuge in him." **(Proverbs 30:5)***

Dear Lord, I thank you for Your Word. It continues to show us that you are our shield, our protector, and our shelter. Thank you Lord for your purified word, which is a lamp to our feet and a light to our paths. Thank you that my husband takes refuge in you and therefore has a shield in you. Your Word declares that every word of God is purified; it's cleansing. May Your Word continue to purify and cleanse us. Thank you for being the shield he didn't know he needed. Teach him how to take refuge in you and show him that he doesn't have to fight every battle.

In the name of Jesus, I pray, Amen.

April 14

"But above all pursue his kingdom and righteousness,
and all these things will be given to you as well."
(Matthew 6:33)

Dear Lord, thank you for the benefits that come with serving and pursuing you. You promise that "all these things" will be given to those who pursue you first. Lord, I thank you for a husband that above all pursues You, Your kingdom, and Your righteousness. Thank you that he is leading our family by example, seeking you first. Thank you for the abundance of "all these things" that are about to manifest in the life of my husband spiritually, mentally, financially, and naturally.

In the name of Jesus, I pray, Amen.

April 15

*"Give, and it will be given to you: A good measure, pressed down, shaken together, running over, will be poured into your lap. For the measure you use will be the measure you receive." **(Luke 6:38)***

Dear Lord, you are the giver of life. You promised a life that is exceeding, abundant, and above all we could ever ask or imagine. Your word declares that givers will be given a good measure, pressed down, shaken together, and running over. Today I pray for my husband to experience all these promises. Give him the capacity to recognize and receive his measure. Thank you for the blessings upon blessings because of his willingness to give. Lord, begin to pour into the lap of my husband.

In the name of Jesus, I pray, Amen.

April 16

"For whoever does the things God wills is My brother and sister and mother!" (Mark 3:35)

Dear Lord, your Word states that it is you who works in us to will and to act according to your good purpose. I thank you, Lord, for a husband whose "food" is to do your will. Thank you for working in him to carry out your good purpose in his life. Minister to him today, clarifying his created purpose, instructing him how to do it and when to do it. He is a man that has been called and set apart to do the things God wills. Lord, continue to be his guide in doing your will. You call him brother. What a beautiful relationship!

In the name of Jesus, I pray, Amen.

April 17

*"Made us alive with Christ even when we were dead in transgressions—it is by grace you have been saved. And God raised us up with Christ and seated us with him in the heavenly realms in Christ Jesus," (**Ephesians 2:5-6**)*

Dear Lord, today I am so grateful for the love, grace, and mercy you have freely given to my husband. I am thankful that my husband has been made alive and therefore seated with you in the heavenly realm. It was your love that raised him from the depths of sin's grave. It was your grace that saved him, and your new mercies daily given, that he can now testify of that salvation. Thank you, Lord, for thinking of him even when he was not thinking about you. Thank you for the authority you have given him to do all things through Christ. Give him the wisdom to operate in that authority daily.

In the name of Jesus, I pray, Amen.

April 18

"No one has seen God at any time. If we love one another,
God resides in us, and his love is perfected in us."
(1 John 4:12)

Dear Lord, your love is the greatest gift given to man. Your love is why we are here today. Thank you for your love. Thank you for the opportunity to love others as ourselves. Lord, I thank you for the love of God that my husband possesses. Thank you for equipping him to love like you've called us to love. Thank you for the Holy Spirit living inside of my husband. Perfect your love in him from day to day and give him the capacity to love like you love. Cancel out the plan of the enemy that has been orchestrated against him to interfere with the way he loves people. Cover him with your blood and with your love, so that he may exude your very nature.

In the name of Jesus, I pray, Amen.

April 19

"For he has rescued us from the kingdom of darkness and transferred us into the Kingdom of his dear Son who purchased our freedom and forgave our sins."
(Colossians 9:13)

Dear Lord, today I want to say thank you for rescuing the life of my husband from the kingdom of darkness. Lord, you have shifted the trajectory of his life with the purchase of his freedom and forgiving his sins. I praise you for all you have done for him, through him, and with him. Thank you for the freedom that has been given to my husband and I cancel the plans of the enemy designed to restrict and restrain him from living out that freedom, in Jesus' name. Continue to minister your freedom to my husband through your word, a song, or the testimony of a friend. Father, you are so good, and your mercy endures forever. I release Your freedom over his life today and every day.

In the name of Jesus, I pray, Amen.

April 20

"But when you give to the needy, do not let your left hand know what your right hand is doing." **(Matthew 6:3)**

Dear Lord, thank you for the bountiful blessings that rest on my husband's life. Thank you for giving him a heart to give. I thank you for a generous husband. May he truly enjoy the gift of giving. Give him your insight on the importance of giving to the needy. May he slow down enough to see the needs of a fallen or broken man. Give him compassion like your son, Jesus. May he operate in humility when giving. Let him not boast or brag because he has blessed someone. May he boast about your goodness and share the love of Christ when presented with the opportunity to bless someone less fortunate.

In the name of Jesus, I pray, Amen.

April 21

*"The point is this: whoever sows sparingly will also reap sparingly, and whoever sows bountifully will also reap bountifully." (**2 Corinthians 9: 6**)*

Dear Lord, thank you for a husband who lives his life based upon the kingdom principles of sowing and reaping. I thank you, Lord, that my husband will sow generously and therefore will reap bountifully. Lord, I thank you that our family will also reap the reward of his obedience. Give him the wisdom to lead us in this kingdom principle so that we can carry out your will on earth as it is in heaven. Thank you for your lavish benefit package. I pray that you would continue to instruct my husband on the significance of sowing and reaping.

In the name of Jesus, I pray, Amen.

April 22

"Each one must give as he has decided in his heart, not reluctantly or under compulsion, for God loves a cheerful giver." (2 Corinthians 9:7)

Dear Lord, I thank you that my husband is a cheerful giver and that he does not give with a clenched fist. Give him divine direction, wisdom, and your heart posture on giving. Teach my husband the importance of being a decisive giver led by the Holy Spirit and not a compulsive giver led by his flesh.

In the name of Jesus, I pray, Amen.

April 23

"One gives freely, yet grows all the richer; another with-holds what he should give, and only suffers want."
(Proverbs 11:24)

Dear Lord, thank you for being a great teacher to my husband. It is your wisdom that instructs us how to "grow all the richer" because we give freely. So, I thank you Lord in advance for a wealthy husband; a husband who has mastered his urges and compulsions to spend in excess. Thank you for giving him wisdom and awareness on how to manage his finances and our finances. I thank you that he is generous and not selfish with his resources. Thank you for a husband that listens and obeys the Holy Spirit.

In the name of Jesus, I pray, Amen.

April 24

"Whoever brings blessing will be enriched, and one who waters will himself be watered." **(Proverbs 11:25)**

Dear Lord, today I am thankful for my husband, a mighty man of valor. He is a man of great spiritual substance, and his presence shifts the atmosphere. Thank you for the authority and influence that my husband possesses. His lifestyle of blessing those around him brings blessings and not curses to him. According to scripture, he "will be enriched" and "himself be watered." His life, finances, friendships, and our marriage are all enriched and watered. Lord, water him with Your Word, love, and grace.

In the name of Jesus, I pray, Amen.

April 25

*"And let us not grow weary of doing good, for in due season we will reap if we do not give up." **(Galatians 6:9)***

Dear Lord, thank you for the peace of God that surpasses all understanding that guards our hearts and minds. Lord, I thank you for the peace that is attainable to him. Today I pray that my husband would not become weary in well-doing. As he continues to do what is right, I pray that you would pour your strength into him. As he strives to do good, renew his mind, body, and soul. Thank you that he has a focused tenacity and unwillingness to quit. When he does feel like giving up, remind him of the promises written in scripture; in due season he will reap if he does not faint and when he is weak your strength is made perfect in him.

In the name of Jesus, I pray, Amen.

April 26

"Though an army encamp against me, my heart shall not fear; though war arise against me, yet I will be confident." (Psalm 27:3)

Dear Lord, thank You for being the great defender and a place of safety for my husband to run and take refuge. You are his strength, and he has no reason to fear when the enemy rises against him. I pray my husband never feels that he is in a battle alone. In any circumstance or situation, give him holy confidence and assurance to know You are right there with him and that You promised to never leave him nor forsake him.

In the name of Jesus, I pray, Amen.

April 27

"One thing I ask from the LORD, this only do I seek: that I may dwell in the house of the LORD all the days of my life; to gaze on the beauty of the LORD and to seek him in his temple." (Psalm 27:4)

Dear Lord, thank you for a husband who seeks you and dwells in your house. Thank you for the access that has been granted to be in constant fellowship and communion with you. Lord, let my husband see the beauty and splendor of knowing you. Bless all the days of the life of my husband. I pray he is always led to find himself in your presence and not in the ways of this world. Thank you that he seeks only to dwell where you are.

In the name of Jesus, I pray, Amen.

April 28

"Teach me your way, O Lord, and lead me on a level path because of my enemies." **(Psalm 27:11)**

Dear Lord, today I declare your word over the life of my husband. In the name of Jesus, I decree and declare that he will learn your way and that he will walk on a level path. Lord, in the areas where he may lack wisdom and insight, clarify Your Word so that he may apply it to the situations of life. As he walks the path you have set for him, make his enemies prepare a table and be at peace with him. Thank you that no weapon formed against him shall prosper and you will silence every voice that rises up to accuse him!

In the name of Jesus, I pray, Amen.

April 29

"I believe that I shall look upon the goodness of the Lord in the land of the living!" **(Psalm 27:13)**

Dear Lord, thank you for my husband's life. Thank you for orchestrating our paths to bring us together. Today I pray that my husband will see your goodness and lovingkindness in the land of the living! Let everywhere that he looks be a reminder of your goodness! Show him your goodness in the trees. Show him your goodness as he passes by water. Show him your goodness as he has positive encounters with people today. Reveal to him the abundant goodness and vibrant life that exists in the land of the living. Remind him that he is alive in you! I pray that you would do the unimaginable in his life, so that he may experience the extravagance of your goodness. Bless his life!

In the name of Jesus, I pray, Amen.

April 30

"...These men, O king, pay no attention to you; they do not serve your gods or worship the golden image that you have set up." (Daniel 3:12b)

Dear Lord, thank you for my husband's bold confession of faith and the choice to live for you. I thank you that he sets his affections on things above and not on the things the world wants him to focus on. Thank you, Lord, that he does not serve or worship idols, but he chooses to only worship You. This single decision shifts the trajectory not only for his life, but for our family, children, and children's children. I declare the plans of Satan have not only been disrupted but they are canceled.

In the name of Jesus, Amen,

MAY

May 1

"Then the king promoted Shadrach, Meshach, and Abed-nego in the province of Babylon." **(Daniel 3:30)**

Dear Lord, today I declare a divine setup for promotion in the life of my husband. Scripture says that promotion comes not from the north, south, east, or west, but it comes from you. Go before him to influence the hearts of men. Thank you for placing my husband in the presence of powerful people setting him up for the greatest testimony of your blessings. Let his reputation of integrity and holiness precede him today so that he stands out and above in his career. I pray your favor on his life will show up today and he will experience a greater harvest. I pray this promotion will be an opportunity to become a blessing to his family and so many others. Lord, get the glory out of his life.

In the name of Jesus, I pray, Amen.

May 2

"So you shall keep the commandments of the Lord your
God by walking in his ways and by fearing him."
(Deuteronomy 8:6)

Dear Lord, I am thankful for a husband who hides
your Word in his heart, keeping your commandments.
It is your Word that will lead and guide him today and
every day. Lord, I thank you for his walk, his talk, and
his attitude that is in reverence to who you are in him.

I pray that he continues to live blamelessly and
unashamed because of his reverence for you. You have
given him the keys to righteousness. Strengthen and
empower him to continue to walk in your ways and to
not stray.

In the name of Jesus, I pray, Amen.

May 3

"For the Lord your God is bringing you into a good land, a land of brooks of water, of fountains and springs, flowing out in the valleys and hills," **(Deuteronomy 8:7)**

Dear Lord, you are God of all, and you are bringing my husband into a good land. It is a land of plenty and not lack. It is a land of life and not death. Thank you for doing a new thing in the life of my husband physically, emotionally, and spiritually. Take my husband's hand and lead him to the place of your goodness. Be his tour guide in the valleys and hills. Today, I declare that my husband has everything because you are bringing him into a good land filled with provision and protection.

In the name of Jesus, I pray, Amen.

May 4

"a land of wheat and barley, of vines and fig trees and pomegranates, a land of olive trees and honey,"
(Deuteronomy 8:8)

Dear Lord, today I continue the prayer of yesterday now asking for your divine presence (olive oil) and the sweetness of your spirit (honey) to overwhelm my husband. Dwell within him so that he will experience the fullness of joy that is found only in your presence. Saturate his mind, his will, and his emotions with your mind, will, and emotions. Let him hunger and thirst for what you desire. I pray that he knows everything that he needs can be found in seeking you. Your Spirit is sweeter than honey on the honeycomb. Pour your sweet Spirit in and through him on today and as he continues to grow. Thank you for the growth and newness of life in my husband.

In the name of Jesus, I pray, Amen.

May 5

"a land in which you will eat bread without scarcity, in which you will lack nothing, a land whose stones are iron, and out of whose hills you can dig copper."
(Deuteronomy 8:9-10)

Dear Lord, thank you for the good land you have blessed my husband to see and experience. You promised to withhold no good thing from him, and you are God who keeps promises. Thank you for being his shepherd, providing guidance, protection, and provision. Lord, it is because of your goodness that my husband has everything he needs, and he is lacking no good thing. Lord, I bless you because my husband is walking into a wealthy place that was divinely designed by You for him. You will be praised by my husband and our family for your interminable goodness.

In the name of Jesus, I pray, Amen.

May 6

"All things were made through Him, and without Him nothing was made that was made." (John 1:3)

Dear Lord, thank you for the beauty and majesty we find in creation. There is nothing that was made, that you didn't have your hand in. Thank you for paying attention to the details of my husband's life. And because you made all things, I just want to take the time today to say thank you Lord for making my husband.

Your Word says he was made through you! That is amazing! And thank you for making him tailor made for me and me for him. Continue to develop us so that we may pour into one another the way you designed.

Without you, there'd be no him. Lead him to grasp the beauty in that he was made through and because of you. I praise you Lord that my husband is fearfully and wonderfully made!

In the name of Jesus, I pray, Amen.

May 7

"In Him was life, and the life was the light of men."
(John 1:4)

Dear Lord, today I bow before You with a grateful heart. Thank you for the precious gift of my husband and the life that is in him. He is a man after Your heart and desires to love only me, his bride, as you have loved your bride. Father, I pray that his expression of love for me will become an example to others of how to love their brides. Let him be the light of men, illuminating the path of righteousness to those around him. I pray grace and blessings are abundant in his life today as he seeks to enrich our life together and the lives of those around him.

In the name of Jesus, I pray, Amen.

May 8

*"And the light shines in the darkness, and the darkness did not comprehend it." **(John 1:5)***

Dear Lord, today I pray for my husband and the elimination of anything trying to delay him. Holy Spirit please reveal those dark places from his past trying to keep him stuck and from the hope and future you promised. Light and darkness cannot dwell together, one must overcome the other. Let there be a supernatural invasion of the territory where darkness tries to hide within my husband and replace it with your light. Fill him daily with the light of your glory so that he can become the light in the darkness.

In the name of Jesus, I pray, Amen.

May 9

"There was a man sent from God, whose name was John." (John 1:6)

Dear Lord, thank you for sending me my husband. He was divinely designed and intentionally created by the Ultimate Creator. Father, I thank you for his uniqueness and the delicate nature of his heart. You made him with his quirky traits just for me. He is not perfect, but he is perfect for me. My husband is the good thing in our family and that is because he knows his value comes from resting in the will of God. He is not good because he is my husband, but because he is your handiwork. You, Lord, created and chose him for such a time as this.

In the name of Jesus, I pray, Amen.

May 10

"This man came for a witness, to bear witness of the Light, that all through him might believe." (John 1:7)

Dear Lord, I honor my husband and his gift to our family. He is a blessing to me in many ways, so it is my greatest pleasure to pray for him daily. Seeking to please you Lord, he is walking in the light of your glory as a man of integrity, honesty, and wisdom. Let all those who will encounter him be able to see Your light shining through his words and his actions. In all that he does, may his life bear witness of You leading the lost to believe in Your power and willingness to save. Today and every day he will reflect God in the earth.

In the name of Jesus, I pray, Amen.

May 11

"And looking to Jesus as He walked, he said, "Behold the Lamb of God!" **(John 1:36)**

Dear Lord, today I pray that my husband will recognize Jesus as the Lamb of God. I pray he finds peace, strength, and guidance in his daily life through his relationship with You. I pray that he can recognize the magnitude of who You are in his life and on the earth. Just as the lamb is meek and humble, Lord I pray that my husband humbly submits to your divine will for his life.

In the name of Jesus, I pray, Amen.

May 12

*"Whenever I am afraid, I will trust you." **(Psalm 56:3)***

Dear Lord, today I pray for my husband to experience
and live in the peace of God that surpasses all understanding. I decree and declare that he is not a man of
fear but of faith. When fear is trying to overwhelm
him, Lord, replace it with the Word of truth. Lord,
remind him that he is not alone and there is no reason
to fear because You are His God. In every challenge
that he faces, in every situation that arises, and in
every circumstance placed before him, you are his
Comforter, his Peace, and You supply him with the
wisdom to make decisions.

In the name of Jesus, I pray, Amen.

May 13

"For since the beginning of the world men have not heard, nor perceived by the ear, neither hath the eye seen, O God, beside thee, what he hath prepared for him that waiteth for him." (Isaiah 64:4)

Dear Lord, I pray for my loving husband today and pray that he may wait patiently for you and trust in your unfailing love and wisdom. May he find comfort and strength in knowing that you are always working for his good, even in times of trial and uncertainty. Lord, his mind can't even conceive all that you have prepared for him because he chooses to wait on you. Thank you for preparing us for one another. Most importantly, thank you for the glory you will receive because of what you have prepared for his life. Thank you for loving my husband the way you do! May he feel that love today! And continue to grant me the grace and wisdom to love, honor and respect him the way you intended me to.

In the name of Jesus, I pray, Amen.

159

May 14

"But when anything is exposed and reproved by the light, it is made visible and clear: and where everything is visible and clear there is light." (Ephesians 5:13)

Dear Lord, order the steps of my husband. Let the light of your glory shine in him and through him. I pray for him to have the courage to walk into dark places and the boldness to expel that darkness with the light of Jesus Christ. Give him spiritual discernment to expose sin but not condemn the sinner. Use my husband to lead them out of their darkness into your redeeming light. Let him be a catalyst for revival at home, in his community, and in the marketplace. I pray a complete hedge of protection all around him and declare that no weapon formed against him will prosper.

In the name of Jesus, I pray, Amen.

May 15

"He says, 'Be still, and know that I am God; I will be exalted among the nations, I will be exalted in the earth.'"
(Psalm 46:10)

Dear Lord, today I pray that my husband finds strength and courage in knowing that you are fighting his battles. Help him to be still and trust in your mighty power, knowing that nothing is too difficult for you. When he faces challenges, give him the confidence to stand firm in his faith. May he find comfort in the knowledge that you are his shield and defender, and that no weapon formed against him shall prosper. As he goes through difficult times, may he experience your peace, which surpasses all understanding. May his heart be filled with joy and confidence in your victory, because you have overcome the world. I declare and decree that my husband is an overcomer!

In the name of Jesus, I pray, Amen.

May 16

"The days are coming," declares the Lord, "when the reaper will be overtaken by the plowman and the planter by the one treading grapes. New wine will drip from the mountains and flow from all the hills," (Amos 9:13)

Dear Lord, I thank you that the days are coming when prosperity will overtake my husband, and the blessings of the Lord will chase him down. Thank you for the new wine in the life of my husband. Let it flow into every area of his life. Leave nothing unstained by the residue of the new wine. Thank you for making all things new and for the revival of dead things. Lord, you get the glory out of his life both now and forever.

In the name of Jesus, I pray, Amen.

May 17

*"Direct my steps by Your word, and let no iniquity have dominion over me." (**Psalm 119:133**)*

Dear Lord, thank you for the gift of my husband, and for the work that you are doing in his life. I pray he continues to walk in obedience, growing in his love for you and in his commitment to follow your will. I decree and declare that the power of generational sin is broken off his life and the lives of our seed. Holy Spirit empower him to resist temptation and to overcome sin. I pray for him to always live a life that is pleasing in your sight and let no iniquity have dominion over him.

In the name of Jesus, I pray, Amen.

May 18

*"But may all who seek you rejoice and be glad in you;
may those who long for your saving help always say,
"The LORD is great!" (Psalm 40:16)*

Dear Lord, you are great! I thank you for my husband and his life being a testimony of your goodness, your grace, and your mercy. You have rescued his life, giving him salvation, and a relationship with you. I pray that my husband will desire to go deeper in his relationship, pursuing you daily with his whole heart. Then he will find satisfaction and fulfillment in your never-ending love and faithfulness. Thank you for blessing me with my husband and establishing Your Word in his life.

In the name of Jesus, I pray, Amen.

May 19

*"And just as you want men to do to you, you also do to them likewise." **(Luke 6:31)***

Dear Lord, thank you for a husband who has a heart that is kind, caring, and empathetic towards others. His kindness for others reflects your love and mercy. He is gracious to the undeserving, loves his neighbors and always shows himself friendly. I thank you that he treats me with compassion and is quick to forgive. I am beyond grateful for a man of God who lives his life to please the Father by loving others well. Lord, I pray that today he is openly rewarded for his lifestyle of loving others well.

In the name of Jesus, I pray, Amen.

May 20

*"But thanks be to God, who gives us the victory through our Lord Jesus Christ." **(1 Corinthians 15:57)***

Dear Lord, thank you that my husband will see the victory that you have already won for him. Thank you, Lord, for sweat-less victories today and every day. Thank you for the battles that he did not have to fight. I praise you Lord for the victory and for my husband being more than a conqueror. Encourage his heart today. Let him walk in the confidence of your power, love, and grace.

In the name of Jesus, I pray, Amen.

May 21

*"But if you do not forgive, neither will your Father in heaven forgive your trespasses." (**Mark 11:26**)*

Dear Lord, thank you for my husband and his willingness to forgive those who have purposely or inadvertently wronged him. I pray that you would heal his heart from any hurts he might have experienced in his childhood, as a youth, and even as an adult. Lord, uproot any seeds of bitterness, grudges, and unforgiveness. Holy Spirit remind him that forgiveness is not about the other person, but it is for him to live a life of freedom.

In the name of Jesus, I pray, Amen.

May 22

"For I, the Lord your God, am a jealous God, visiting the iniquity of the fathers upon the children to the third and fourth generations of those who hate Me, but showing mercy to thousands, to those who love Me and keep My commandments." **(Deuteronomy 5:9b-10)**

Dear Lord, thank you for my husband who has been given the power to break generational curses. I decree and declare that the power of sin is broken over his life and that every generational curse be broken over the lives of our family members. Thank you for the blood of Jesus that was shed to break the curse of sin and death. May my husband walk in the Spirit on all occasions and continue to deny the desires of his flesh. Continue to show him mercy because he loves you, he obeys you and he is faithful to keep your command-ments.

In the name of Jesus, I pray, Amen.

May 23

"The soul of the sluggard craves and gets nothing, while the soul of the diligent is richly supplied."
(Proverbs 13:4)

Dear Lord, thank you for a husband who is not lazy but is diligent. He is creative, productive, and a wise manager of time. My husband is a mighty man of valor and honesty. My husband is a dependable leader in our family, faithful to the ministry, and consistent in his job. Lord, I pray that you would give him the desires of his heart and reward him for his unfailing diligence.

In the name of Jesus, I pray, Amen.

May 24

"Therefore, if you have been raised with Christ [to a new life, sharing in His resurrection from the dead], keep seeking the things that are above, where Christ is, seated at the right hand of God." (Colossians 3:1)

Dear Lord, I am blessed to have my husband who has been born again and he is a new creation in you. Thank you that his spirit has been resurrected to a new life and he is no longer dead to sin. When the enemy tries to remind him of his old life, let there be a quickening in his spirit to remind him that all old things have passed away. Lord, I am thankful that you are seated at the right hand of the Father. I pray for the focus of my husband and that he will seek the things that are above.

In the name of Jesus, I pray, Amen.

May 25

"Set your mind and keep focused habitually on the things above [the heavenly things], not on things that are on the earth [which have only temporal value]."
(Colossians 3:2)

Dear Lord, I praise you for being the King of kings and the Lord of lords. Everything we need is in you. Thank you for meeting my husband's every need. With so many distractions in the world, and particularly his world, I pray that you would give him the will and strength to keep his mind stayed on you and on heavenly things. Help him to think on things that are noble, right, pure, lovely, and admirable. Make him to know the depth, value and gift of eternal life with you. Thank you that his focus is not on temporary things, but on things that have an everlasting impact.

In the name of Jesus, I pray, Amen.

May 26

"For you died [to this world], and your [new, real] life is hidden with Christ in God. When Christ, who is our life, appears, then you also will appear with Him in glory."
(Colossians 3:3-4)

Dear Lord, thank you for my husband who is hidden in you and has found his identity in you. Thank you that he has decided to live for you and put to death his old nature, habits, and ways of thinking. He is looking more like you, his ways are like yours and his thoughts are like yours. As he continues to seek your ways, Lord, empower him to lead our family with courage and the wisdom of your will, according to your Word. I pray that he experiences the fullness of your joy as he chooses to live his life for your glory.

In the name of Jesus, I pray, Amen.

May 27

"So put to death and deprive of power the evil longings of your earthly body [with its sensual, self-centered instincts] immorality, impurity, sinful passion, evil desire, and greed, which is [a kind of] idolatry [because it replaces your devotion to God]."
(Colossians 3:5)

Dear Lord, I praise you for the power that we have through the working of the Holy Spirit. I pray that my husband is a man of pure intent and free from sexual immorality and idolatry. Thank you for a selfless man who worships you in spirit and in truth. I pray that you would continue to enable him to stay pure before you. Dear Lord, where he feels weak or ashamed because of any sexual, immoral or impure struggles, I pray that you would lift the scales from his eyes and minister to his spirit. Let him know that there is no condemnation to those who are in Christ Jesus. Lead him to seek deliverance and not to cover those sins. Grant the space for us to be able to communicate about areas of weakness with wisdom, love and understanding.

In the name of Jesus, I pray, Amen.

May 28

*"But now rid yourselves [completely] of all these things: anger, rage, malice, slander, and obscene (abusive, filthy, vulgar) language from your mouth." **(Colossians 3:8)***

Dear Lord, I thank you for my husband who loves me according to your Word. Thank you Lord for a husband who speaks peace. Thank you that his speech is uplifting, cleansing and encouraging. May the words that come from his mouth be acceptable in your sight.

Lord, I pray that when he is tempted to operate in malice, your Spirit would rise up in him to guide him to a more godly response.

In the name of Jesus, I pray, Amen.

May 29

*"Do not lie to one another, for you have stripped off the old self with its evil practices," **(Colossians 3:9)***

Dear Lord, your design for marriage is our blueprint for success. Thank you for my husband who seeks to have a true and loving relationship with his bride. The enemy desires to kill, steal, and to destroy our marriage with deception and dishonesty. Father, I pray for my husband and our marriage. I come against any plan, plot, and scheme the enemy has devised to wreak havoc in our home. He will not succeed and together we will live the abundant life you have promised.

In the name of Jesus, I pray, Amen.

May 30

"And have put on the new [spiritual] self who is being continually renewed in true knowledge in the image of Him who created the new self—" **(Colossians 3:10)**

Dear Lord, I come to you in humble submission on behalf of my husband. I pray that you would renew my husband in true knowledge each day. There are many organizations, cults and groups made, not in the image of Christ, which seek to sift those who are desperate and looking for answers. I pray that you would cover my husband's mind with your blood and give him spiritual discernment to not fall into those traps. I pray that he walks confidently in and understands more and more his new identity in you. Thank you for the true knowledge of who you are. May he aspire and be motivated to walk in the newness of who you created him to be.

In the name of Jesus, I pray, Amen.

May 31

"So, as God's own chosen people, who are holy [set apart, sanctified for His purpose] and well-beloved [by God Himself], put on a heart of compassion, kindness, humility, gentleness, and patience [which has the power to endure whatever injustice or unpleasantness comes, with good temper];" **(Colossians 3:12)**

Dear Lord, thank you for my husband, whom you have chosen to be holy and sanctified. He is filled with compassion, kindness, humility, and gentleness. Lord, I want to thank you for this wonderful gift you have given to me. My husband is undeniably different and has been set apart, not just for me but for your purposes. I pray for a daily manifestation of the fruit of the spirit in his life.

In the name of Jesus, I pray, Amen.

JUNE

June 1

"bearing graciously with one another, and willingly forgiving each other if one has a cause for complaint against another; just as the Lord has forgiven you, so should you forgive." (Colossians 3:13)

Dear Lord, thank you for the gift of forgiveness. Lord, today, even if I don't see it manifesting in my marriage, I speak life and I thank you for a marriage where we bear graciously with one another. Thank you that we both lead with love and forgiveness. Teach us how to communicate effectively and settle matters in a godly manner. Give us the capacity to forgive just as you have forgiven us. Lord where unforgiveness is hidden, I pray you would reveal it so that we may walk in truth and in love. Show us where we may be harboring unforgiveness. We don't want unforgiveness to block the free flow of your Holy Spirit. So, I pray for supernatural strength to forgive one another just as you have forgiven us.

In the name of Jesus, I pray, Amen.

June 2

*"Beyond all these things put on and wrap yourselves in [unselfish] love, which is the perfect bond of unity [for everything is bound together in agreement when each one seeks the best for others]." (**Colossians 3:14**)*

Dear Lord, I am so grateful for your love. It's indescribable. And today my prayer is that you would wrap us both with unselfish love. Help us to seek out the best for one another and others. Forgive us for operating in self-centeredness. Wash us with your blood and teach us how to love unselfishly. We want to look like you in our love for one another and walk in the bond of unity, which commands a blessing. Deepen our love for you, Lord, and then for one another.

In the name of Jesus, I pray, Amen.

June 3

"Let the peace of Christ [the inner calm of one who walks daily with Him] be the controlling factor in your hearts [deciding and settling questions that arise]. To this peace indeed you were called as members in one body [of believers]. And be thankful [to God always]."
(Colossians 3:15)

Dear Lord, thank you for a peace that is available to my husband who walks with you daily. I pray that my husband will keep his mind on you, and you will give him the promise of perfect peace. I thank you for peace being the foundation and the soundtrack of our marriage. When there are disagreements, let peace always be the deciding and settling factor.

In the name of Jesus, I pray, Amen.

June 4

*"Let the word of Christ dwell in you richly in all wisdom,
teaching and admonishing one another in psalms and hymns
and spiritual songs, singing with grace in your hearts to the
Lord." **(Colossians 3:16)***

Dear Lord, I lift up my beloved husband to you today and ask that you fill him with the wisdom and knowledge of your Word. I pray that your Word would have its home in my husband's heart so that he may be filled with your peace and truth. Give him the wisdom to be the leader and a teacher in our marriage and home. May he be guided by your Holy Spirit in all that he does, and may he use his gifts and talents to glorify your name. May he find delight in teaching and encouraging others using wisdom with gratitude in his heart. Help our marriage to be rooted in your Word and to grow in love and unity, so that we may live together in harmony with your will.

In the name of Jesus, I pray, Amen.

June 5

"Whatever you do [no matter what it is] in word or deed, do everything in the name of the Lord Jesus [and in dependence on Him], giving thanks to God the Father through Him." **(Colossians 3:17)**

Dear Lord, I pray that you would teach my husband to have total dependence on you, giving thanks to you through Jesus Christ. Let him lean not on his own understanding, but in all his ways acknowledge you. May every word and every action be spoken and done with a heart of thanksgiving and a desire to honor you. Help him to use his talents and abilities to bring glory to Your Name and to bless those around him. Let his work, love, and everything that he does, be done in Your Name. Bless him with your favor in all of his endeavors. May our marriage be a testament of your love and grace, and may it bring glory to Your Name.

In the name of Jesus, I pray, Amen.

June 6

"Wives, be subject to your husbands [out of respect for their position as protector, and their accountability to God], as is proper and fitting in the Lord."
(Colossians 3:18)

Dear Lord, thank you for placing the desire in me to be a godly wife. Thank you for choosing me to be my husband's helper. Prepare me and continue to develop me into the wife you've called me to be. Help me to submit to his leadership as he submits to you. I thank you for a husband who has submitted his life to your authority. I am grateful for a man of God who is faithful to the vow promising to love, honor, and cherish me so long as we both shall live. Fix my heart to be subject to him, trusting that you have chosen him to be my protector. Help me to trust him and to trust the Holy Spirit in him.

In the name of Jesus, I pray, Amen.

June 7

"Husbands, love your wives [with an affectionate, sympathetic, selfless love that always seeks the best for them] and do not be embittered or resentful toward them [because of the responsibilities of marriage]."
(Colossians 3:19)

Dear Lord, I submit my life to you. Teach me how to be a wife to my husband. Show me how to love him right where he is. I never want to be harsh or insensitive towards him, but affectionate and empathetic to his needs. I want to love him the way you love him, desiring only him. Lord, give me the words to build up his confidence, encouraging him to be the husband you created. I am his helper. I pray for him, and he prays for me. I honor the covenant vow finding great pleasure in being his wife and the responsibilities of marriage.

In the name of Jesus, I pray, Amen.

June 8

*"Therefore, be patient, brethren, until the coming of the Lord. See how the farmer waits for the precious fruit of the earth, waiting patiently for it until it receives the early and latter rain." (**James 5:7**)*

Dear Lord, I praise you today simply because you are good and your mercy endures forever. We are so undeserving, but I praise you that our lives speak of your goodness. I pray for my god-fearing husband today. I pray that you would continue to give him the desire to operate in the fruit of the spirit. Today I pray for his patience. I praise you that he doesn't make moves hastily. And I thank you that he moves with grace and wisdom. Let him not be stirred up when things don't go as planned. Give him grace to deal with inconveniences and allow that grace to develop his character in you. Show him the virtue of patiently waiting until he receives the latter rain in his life.

In the name of Jesus, I pray, Amen.

June 9

"So be strong and courageous, all you who put your hope in the Lord!" (Psalm 31:24)

Dear Lord, I come to you boldly today in prayer for my awesome and loving husband. I pray that in a world where hopelessness is all around, my husband wholeheartedly puts his hope in you first! Let him not put his trust in temporal things, but in all his ways acknowledge you. Where he is lacking in hope, fill him with a fresh batch. Renew his strength. May he walk and not be weary, may he run and not faint. Thank you for his courageousness. May the joy of the Lord be his strength. Not just today, but for the rest of his life!

In the name of Jesus, I pray, Amen.

June 10

"Therefore, come out from among them and be separate, says the Lord. Do not touch what is unclean, and I will receive you." (2 Corinthians 6:17)

Dear Lord, thank you for my husband who chooses to be separate and does not touch what is unclean. He is not satisfied by the various temptations of this world. My husband has a pure heart and clean hands. May his life be pleasing in your sight as he continues to turn from the ways of the wicked. He does not walk, stand, or sit in the way of the ungodly. My husband delights in your Word and meditates on it day and night. He is a man after your heart. Thank you for receiving his heart. You are his and he is yours.

In the name of Jesus, I pray, Amen.

June 11

*"For God so loved the world that He gave His only begot-
ten Son, that whoever believes in Him should not perish
but have everlasting life."* **(John 3:16)**

Dear Lord, I thank you for the gift of everlasting life
that you have given to those who believe in you. I
praise you for being the ultimate sacrifice and example of love. Because my husband believes in you, I
thank you that he has found everlasting life in you.
Teach him that he doesn't have to wait until eternity
to walk in this promise. May he know what it feels like
to walk with you daily in the kingdom of God. Thank
you that his destiny is set and that he has found everlasting life in you. Always remind him of this promise
whenever he feels defeated. I declare and decree that
my husband is more than a conqueror through Christ
Jesus!

In the name of Jesus, I pray, Amen.

June 12

"But let none of you suffer as a murderer, a thief, an evil-doer, or as a busybody in other people's matters."
(1 Peter 4:15)

Dear Lord, thank you for the purpose you have for my husband. He is always about his Father's business and has no time to meddle in the matters of people's affairs. I thank you that he is not a murderer with his words, a thief of peace, or an evildoer seeking to harm others. He is a good man who does good things for me, for his family, his friends, and his community. I thank you that his mind is stable and not double-minded. Distractions come, but he is focused on things above and fulfilling the plan of God for his life.

In the name of Jesus, I pray, Amen.

June 13

*"Let your conduct be without covetousness; be content with such things as you have. For He Himself has said: I will never leave you nor forsake you." **(Hebrews 13:5)***

Dear Lord, my husband is a blessed man. He has a wife that loves him, a family that respects him, and a community that speaks well of him. I thank you that he does not compare, but he is content in Christ. I praise you that he is not jealous of others, but rejoices with those who rejoice. He does not covet but praises you for all that you have given him. Thank you for supplying all his needs and loading him up with benefits daily, adding no sorrow.

In the name of Jesus, I pray, Amen.

June 14

*"Brethren, I do not count myself to have apprehended; but one thing I do, forgetting those things which are behind and reaching forward to things which are ahead. I press toward the goal for the prize of the upward call of God in Christ Jesus." **(Philippians 3:13)***

Dear Lord, I come to you with a grateful heart thanking you for the gift of my husband. I thank you for a forward thinking husband, who is not stuck on past hurts, disappointments and failures, but hopeful and confident about his future. I declare that he is free. I declare that he will walk in his freedom and in his upward call in you. Help him to let go of any past hurts or mistakes, and to look towards the future with hope and a renewed sense of purpose. May our marriage be a reflection of your love and grace, and may we continue to grow in our faith together.

In the name of Jesus, I pray, Amen.

June 15

"Grace and peace [that special sense of spiritual well-being] be multiplied to you in the [true, intimate] knowledge of God and of Jesus our Lord." **(2 Peter 1:2)**

Dear Lord, today I thank and praise you for your grace and peace in my husband's life, mind, body, and spirit. I pray that you would multiply his peace today. Whatever he may be facing, I pray that he rests in the knowledge of who you are and that he feels you near.

Father, I pray that you would continue to take him deeper, giving him more revelation and knowledge of your Word. Where there are mind-binding thoughts that would hinder his comprehension of who you are, I bind those thoughts and take authority over them in the name of Jesus. Lord, release a divine clarity of the Word of God in my husband's life. I declare he will speak about your Word with boldness and authority.

In the name of Jesus, I pray, Amen.

June 16

"He who believes in Me [who adheres to, trusts in, and relies on Me], as the Scripture has said, 'From his innermost being will flow continually rivers of living water."
(John 7:38)

Dear Lord, I thank you that your Word is true! And that it will not lie! This means that because my husband believes in you, as the Scripture has said, rivers of living water will flow from his heart! I thank you that my husband adheres to you and that he trusts in and relies not on man or things, but in and on you! I pray for that river to begin to manifest from his innermost being and that it will flow continually! Let it flow, Lord, from his mouth, in our home, in our marriage and his life. I pray he continues to trust, depend, and rely on you and you alone.

In the name of Jesus, I pray, Amen.

June 17

"Brethren, do not be children in understanding; however, in malice be babes, but in understanding be mature."
(1 Corinthians 14:20)

Dear Lord, I lift up my beloved husband to you today, wherever he may be in this world. I thank you for a mature husband who desires to be a man of understanding. I thank you that when the temptation comes for him to be malicious, his response is that of a baby; quick to forgive and giving in love. I thank you for your unconditional love that flows from my husband and through our marriage. Thank you that in all his getting, he gets understanding; that's Your Word! Let immaturity and selfishness have no place in our marriage. Continuously remind us to prefer the other above ourselves. May we be "babe-like" in our marriage, not keeping records of wrong. Let your love flow in and through us.

In the name of Jesus, I pray, Amen.

June 18

"For our light affliction, which is but for a moment, is working for us a far more exceeding and eternal weight of glory." **(2 Corinthians 4:17)**

Dear Lord, thank You for my husband that turns to you when he is faced with challenges. He is not thrown off when affliction comes. When times are unpredictable and seasons are difficult, he presses into you even more. Scripture affirms his afflictions are momentary and light, there is a greater glory, and nothing he goes through compares to what you have endured for him. I pray that my husband will grasp this word for his life and will always maintain this spiritual mindset.

In the name of Jesus, I pray, Amen.

June 19

"So we look not at the things which are seen, but at the things which are unseen; for the things which are visible are temporal [just brief and fleeting], but the things which are invisible are everlasting and imperishable."
(2 Corinthians 4:18)

Dear Lord, I pray that my husband will be a man of divine focus. Thank you that he is not distracted by the things of this world, but that he understands the value in the spiritual and eternal. Enlighten him and teach him that whatever he can see with his natural eye, there is spiritual significance behind it. Grant him tunnel vision to the things of you. When the enemy arises to distract him, gently remind him of his end goal in Christ; and grant him the strength to overcome.

In the name of Jesus, I pray, Amen.

June 20

"For you were bought at a price; therefore glorify God in your body and in your spirit which are God's."
(1 Corinthians 6:20)

Dear Lord, thank you for purchasing us at a price we will never be able to repay. I praise you for all the benefits we inherit because of your sacrifice. Our bodies and our spirits are yours. Today I pray that you would strengthen, encourage and empower my husband to glorify you in his body and in his spirit. As he walks, talks and works, allow your Spirit to rise up in him, so that men will see his works, but that you get the glory! May his words, actions and deeds line up with your Word and may everything attached to him be blessed.

In the name of Jesus, I pray, Amen.

June 21

"Pride goes before destruction, and a haughty spirit before a fall. Better to be of a humble spirit with the lowly, than to divide the spoil with the proud."
(Proverbs 16:18-19)

Dear Lord, there is nothing like a man of humility. You are the ultimate example of humility. Thank you that my husband desires to be like you in every way. Thank you that he has a humble spirit and that he denies his flesh daily. I pray Lord that you would so graciously reveal to him any areas in his life where pride resides, and he is unaware. Pride goes before destruction. I pray for the opposite in my husband's life. I pray for humility that will lead to divine creation, building, and construction because he despises pride and walks in humility like you, Jesus.

In the name of Jesus, I pray, Amen.

June 22

*"Do not judge and criticize and condemn [others unfairly with an attitude of self-righteous superiority as though assuming the office of a judge], so that you will not be judged [unfairly]." **(Matthew 7:1)***

Dear Lord, I come to you today with a grateful heart for my husband. Thank you for the opportunity to pray for him and to keep him covered in prayer. I sincerely pray that you would help me not to judge, criticize or condemn my husband, especially when I do not agree or understand what he is doing. Give me understanding and insight into the work that you are doing in his life. Help me to operate in love and mercy. I also thank you that my husband is full of love and mercy. Thank you that with each day, he is looking more and more like you. I pray that he is fair and respectful with others and that he does not take the seat of a judge, but rather the seat of one who understands that mercy triumphs over judgment.

In the name of Jesus, I pray, Amen.

June 23

"Blessed be the God and Father of our Lord Jesus Christ! According to his great mercy, he has caused us to be born again to a living hope through the resurrection of Jesus Christ from the dead," **(1 Peter 1:3)**

Dear Lord, you are blessed and worthy to be praised! I thank you for the living hope my husband has because he has been born again. Thank you for your resurrection, which gives us power over the enemy. According to your great mercy, which we do not deserve, you caused us to be born again to a living hope through the resurrection of Jesus Christ from the dead. Because He rose, our spirits are resurrected. We are no longer dead to our sins. May my husband rest and walk boldly in the gift you bestowed to him according to your great mercy - eternal life, and a living hope. Thank you, Jesus!

In the name of Jesus, I pray, Amen.

June 24

*"I know your deeds, that you are neither cold nor hot. I wish you were either one or the other! So, because you are lukewarm—neither hot nor cold—I am about to spit you out of my mouth." **(Revelation 3:15-16)***

Dear Lord, I thank you for a husband that is on fire for you! I declare and decree that my husband develops a passion for you and for the things of you. I pray he finds purpose in pursuing the things of Christ. I pray he finds fulfillment in serving you. Fill his voids with your presence, because in your presence is the fullness of joy. Lord, when he begins to get comfortable or stagnant, nudge his heart to return to you again; to stay on fire for you! Lord, I pray for a marriage that is hot for you! May we exude you in everything we do!

In the name of Jesus, I pray, Amen.

June 25

*"And whoever does not carry their cross and follow me cannot be my disciple." **(Luke 14:27)***

Dear Lord, I thank you for a husband that chooses to pick up his cross daily and follows you. Thank you that his food is to do your will. I pray for a husband that has the discipline and the desire to be a learner of you. Guide him in making decisions that are in line with your will and help him to discern what is important in life. Help him to embrace the challenges and sacrifices that come with being a faithful follower of Jesus. Thank you for the sacrifice that Jesus made on the cross, and for the example that he set for all of us. I pray that my husband will follow his footsteps and live a life of faith and obedience.

In the name of Jesus, I pray, Amen.

June 26

"For God alone, my soul waits in silence and quietly submits to Him, For my hope is from Him." **(Psalm 62:5)**

Dear Lord, thank you for being a God who is worthy of our trust and confidence. I praise you Lord for a husband that is content to wait in silence for you. Remind him to place his hope in you in times of uncertainty or difficulty and that he can rely on you in all circumstances. Help him to cast his worries, anxieties, and concerns upon you, knowing that you care for him. Whatever challenges he may face today, I pray that you would help him to recognize that you are his rock, his salvation, and his fortress. I pray he experiences your loving presence in a new and profound way. I pray that my husband will find his rest and security in you alone.

In the name of Jesus, I pray, Amen.

June 27

*"He only is my rock and my salvation; He is my defense;
I shall not be moved." **(Psalm 62:6)***

Dear Lord, thank you for being a God who is faithful
and true, and for your unwavering love for us. Thank
you, Lord, for being my husband's rock and salvation.
When everything around him is unwavering and un-
steady, thank you for being his constant. Thank you
for being my husband's great Defender! Teach him to
stand steadfast and immovable. I ask that you surround him with your protection and love. I pray he is a
shining example of your love and grace to those
around him. I pray that my husband would find his
refuge and hope in you alone.

In the name of Jesus, I pray, Amen.

June 28

"In God is my salvation and my glory; the rock of my strength, and my refuge is in God." **(Psalm 62:7)**

Dear Lord, thank you for your faithfulness and love, and for the gift of salvation that you offer to all who trust in you. I pray for my husband and ask that you would lead him to find his salvation and glory in you, in every area of his life. Help him to always trust in you, and to seek your guidance and wisdom in all that he does. I pray he is not swayed by the opinions or desires of others, but instead, be rooted in your truth and led by your Spirit. Help him to recognize your presence with him, and to take comfort in your promises. I ask that you bless him with your favor and protection and guide him along the path that you have set for him. I pray he walks in the fullness of your joy and purpose and is a beacon of your light to those around him.

In the name of Jesus, I pray, Amen.

June 29

"But the Lord answered and said unto her, Martha,
Martha, thou art anxious and troubled about many
things: but one thing is needful: for Mary hath chosen the
good part, which shall not be taken away from her."
(Luke 10:41-42)

Dear Lord, I pray for my husband and ask that he
would follow the example of Mary, who chose to sit at
your feet and listen to your teaching. I pray he priori-
tizes his relationship with you above all else and finds
his rest and peace in your presence. When he is distracted by the worries and pressures of life, help him
to recognize the importance of seeking wisdom and
guidance. I pray he has a heart that is open to your
teaching and a mind that is receptive to your truth.
Help him to grow in his faith and knowledge of you,
developing a more intimate relationship with you.

In the name of Jesus, I pray, Amen.

June 30

*"Create in me a clean heart, O God, and renew a steadfast spirit within me." (**Psalm 51:10**)*

Dear Lord, thank you for the work that you are doing in my husband's life. I lift him up to you today and ask that you would create in him a clean heart. I pray he seeks your forgiveness and grace and turns away from anything that separates him from you. I pray he be filled with your Holy Spirit and have a heart that is open to your leading and guidance. Help him to grow in his love for you and in his desire to live a life that pleases you. When he falls short or makes mistakes, I pray he finds comfort and strength in your grace and mercy. I pray he seeks your forgiveness and be quick to repent, knowing that you are faithful to forgive and to cleanse us from all unrighteousness. May his heart be pure and his intentions honorable. I pray he be a man of integrity, whose thoughts, words, and actions are pleasing to you.

In the name of Jesus, I pray, Amen.

JULY

July 1

"God is Spirit, and those who worship Him must worship in spirit and truth." **(John 4:24)**

Dear Lord, Thank you for the gift of worship. I praise you and worship you. You are holy. You are worthy. You are a Mighty God. Hallelujah to your Name. Lord, I pray for my husband and thank you that he worships you in spirit and truth. I thank you that he is sincere and genuine in his worship. May his heart and mind be fully focused on you. Help him to recognize your presence in his life daily, and to approach you with reverence and humility. I pray he grows in his understanding of your truth and your ways and be guided by your Holy Spirit in all that he does. I pray he finds joy and peace in his worship of you, and may his life reflect your love and grace. I pray that as my husband worships you in spirit and truth, and experience the fullness of your presence in his life.

In the name of Jesus, I pray, Amen.

July 2

*"He has shown you, O man, what is good; and what does the Lord require of you but to do justly, to love mercy, and to walk humbly with your God?" **(Micah 6:8)***

Dear Lord, thank you for showing us what is good. You are good and your mercy endures forever! I thank you that my husband acts justly, loves mercy, and walks humbly with you. I pray he seeks to do what is right and fair, showing compassion and kindness to others, and always acknowledges his dependence on you. Help him to follow your ways and to trust in your guidance, so that he may live a life that is pleasing to you and bring glory to your name.

In the name of Jesus, I pray, Amen.

July 3

"Trust in the Lord with all your heart, and lean not on your own understanding; in all your ways acknowledge Him, and He shall direct your paths." **(Proverbs 3:5-6)**

Dear Lord, I thank you that my husband places all his trust in you. Thank you that he acknowledges you in all his ways, seeking your guidance and wisdom in every decision he makes. Help him to have faith in your plan for his life, even when it is difficult or unclear. I pray he will find peace and security in knowing that you will direct his path and lead him toward your perfect will. I praise you that his interest is in following you. Direct his path, dear Lord. Be a lamp to his feet and a light to his pathway.

In the name of Jesus, I pray, Amen.

July 4

"Be anxious for nothing, but in everything by prayer and supplication, with thanksgiving, let your requests be made known to God" **(Philippians 4:6)**

Dear Lord, on this Independence Day, I thank and praise you for the freedom we have in you. Today I pray for my husband to experience the peace that transcends all understanding that comes from you alone. Help him to not be anxious about anything, but in every situation, by prayer and petition, with thanksgiving, I pray he presents his requests to you. I pray he trusts that you hear his prayers and will provide all his needs by your perfect will. Strengthen him and fill him with your peace and help him to trust in your goodness and faithfulness, knowing that you are always with him.

In the name of Jesus, I pray, Amen.

July 5

"Blessed and greatly favored is the man whose strength is in You, In whose heart are the highways to Zion."
(Psalm 84:5)

Dear Lord, thank you for your many blessings and favor in our lives. Today I pray that you would bless my husband and fill him with supernatural strength. As he walks through this journey of life, I pray he finds his strength in you and sets his heart in pursuit of your holy presence. I pray he finds joy in your house and draws closer to you each day, trusting in your unwavering love and provision. May you grant him favor with you God and favor with men. Help him to persevere through any challenges he may face today, and may your peace be his guide always.

In the name of Jesus, I pray, Amen.

July 6

"The grace of the Lord Jesus Christ, and the love of God, and the communion of the Holy Spirit be with you all. Amen." (2 Corinthians 13:14)

Dear Lord, I pray that you would fill my husband with your grace, love, and fellowship. May your grace be with him in every situation he faces, and I pray he feels your never-ending love guiding and protecting him. Help him to grow in fellowship with you and with others, experiencing the unity and peace that comes from your presence. I pray that he may be strengthened by the Holy Spirit as he goes throughout his day, always trusting in the love of Christ.

In the name of Jesus, I pray, Amen.

July 7

"And do not be conformed to this world, but be transformed by the renewing of your mind, that you may prove what is that good and acceptable and perfect will of God." **(Romans 12:2)**

Dear Lord, I pray that you would renew my husband's mind and transform him from the inside out. Help him to see the world through your eyes and to discern your will for his life. Protect him from the negative influence of the world and guide him towards your truth and righteousness. Eliminate the lies the enemy has planted that hinder him from forward movement in you. I pray that his heart and mind will continually be renewed by your Spirit, so that he may walk in your perfect will and bring glory to your name.

In the name of Jesus, I pray, Amen."

July 8

"And in all things show yourself to be an example of good works, with purity in doctrine [having the strictest regard for integrity and truth], dignified," **(Titus 2:7)**

Dear Lord, I pray that you would help my husband to be a shining example of good works, demonstrating purity in his lifestyle and a commitment to truth and integrity. Please guide him as he leads and interacts with others, giving him wisdom and discernment to navigate any challenges or distractions that come his way. I pray he is gracious in his conduct, with a heart that is wholly devoted to you. I pray that his words and actions will reflect your love and grace and that he will bring glory to your name in all that he does.

In the name of Jesus, I pray, Amen.

July 9

"And not only that, but we also glory in tribulations, knowing that tribulation produces perseverance; and perseverance, character; and character, hope."
(Romans 5:3-4)

Dear Lord, what a perspective to have! That we can glory in tribulation! My prayer for my husband today is that when he faces tribulation, his perspective is shifted towards you. I pray that you would strengthen him in his faith and give him the courage to face any challenge with hope and grace. May his character be refined through these trials, and may he grow in his reliance on you. I pray that he would find joy in the midst of suffering, knowing that your love and grace are sufficient to sustain him. May his testimony inspire others to trust in your goodness and faithfulness.

Give him a fresh hope. Encourage his soul.

In the name of Jesus, I pray, Amen.

July 10

"Because we are united with Christ, we have received an inheritance from God, for he chose us in advance, and he makes everything work out according to his plan."
(Ephesians 1:11)

Dear Lord, thank you for the blessing of being united with you. Thank you for choosing my husband. Thank you for having your hand on his life, making everything work according to your plan and purpose. I thank you that you have already predestined and marked out his path, and I pray that he would have a heart willing to follow that path, even if it is difficult. Please help him to trust in your sovereignty and to know that you have a purpose for every circumstance and situation he faces. I pray that he walks confidently in his calling and is a beacon of your love and grace to those around him. I pray he is filled with your wisdom and discernment so he can make the best decisions for himself and our family.

In the name of Jesus, I pray, Amen.

221

July 11

"In a similar way urge the young men to be sensible and self-controlled and to behave wisely [taking life seriously]." **(Titus 2:6)**

Dear Lord, I pray for a sensible husband, a mature man of faith. I pray that he has self-control and uses wisdom daily. Thank you, Lord, that my husband is thoughtful and wise in his decision-making. Please give him the strength and discipline to resist any temptation that would avert him from your will. Help him to be grounded in your truth and wisdom, and a living example of your grace and love. I pray that you would place other godly men around him that are good examples for him. I pray he is a blessing to our family, friends, and those in our community who need to see your light shining through him. Thank you for my husband and for the gifts and talents that you have given him. May he use them for your glory and honor.

In the name of Jesus, I pray, Amen.

July 12

"Now you have diligently followed [my example, that is]
my teaching, conduct, purpose, faith, patience, love,
steadfastness," (2 Timothy 3:10)

Dear Lord, I thank you for a husband that diligently
follows your teaching. His conduct, faith, patience,
love, and steadfastness are tangible evidence of how
closely he follows you. As he continues to follow you
and to lead our family, I pray that you would help him
to be steadfast and persistent in his faith. I pray that
he would be diligent in reading and studying your
Word and that he would be quick to apply it to his life.
Please help him to resist the temptations and distractions that can so easily lead him astray, and to be focused on the will and purpose of his life. May his testimony be a powerful witness to the transforming
power of your gospel.

In the name of Jesus, I pray, Amen.

July 13

*"For it is God who works in you both to will and to do for His good pleasure." **(Philippians 2:13)***

Dear Lord, I pray that even today you would work within my husband to bring about your purpose in his life. I know you have put passions and desires in him to carry out your will on the earth, through his life. I pray that he would be open to your leadership and that he would have a heart that desires to do your will. Grant him the courage to execute the ideas, dreams, and visions you have planted in his heart and mind throughout his life. I pray he be filled with your Spirit and guided by your wisdom to carry out your plan for his life. May his life reflect your goodness and grace, and I pray he experiences the fullness of your joy and peace as he walks in obedience to your will.

In the name of Jesus, I pray, Amen.

July 14

"Now fear the Lord and serve him with all faithfulness. Throw away the gods your ancestors worshiped beyond the Euphrates River and in Egypt, and serve the Lord."
(Joshua 24:14)

Dear Lord, I thank you today that my husband fears you. Thank you for a husband that serves you in sincerity and truth. And because he is faithful in serving you, he is faithful in serving others. Continue to give him the strength to say no to the temptation of worshiping the gods of his ancestors, father, and grandfather. When he is distracted, always direct his heart back to you. Reveal to him how easy it is to make an idol out of something and give him the resolve to stand firm in his decision to worship you alone. I thank you for the fear that he has for you and that he serves you with all faithfulness.

In the name of Jesus, I pray, Amen.

July 15

"But if serving the Lord seems undesirable to you, then choose for yourselves this day whom you will serve, whether the gods your ancestors served beyond the Euphrates, or the gods of the Amorites, in whose land you are living. But as for me and my household, we will serve the Lord." (Joshua 24:15)

Dear Lord, I come before you today thanking you for my husband and for continuing to shape him into the man of God you called him to be. I pray that you would give him boldness like Joshua to choose you. I praise you for a godly leader in our home that chooses you for himself which allows me to follow him as he follows you. I thank you that serving you is desirable and fulfilling for him. Breathe on his decisions so that they continue to guide him, and everyone connected to him. I declare and decree that everyone in my household will serve the Lord!

In the name of Jesus, I pray, Amen.

July 16

"In conclusion, be strong in the Lord [draw your strength from Him and be empowered through your union with Him] and in the power of His [boundless] might."
(Ephesians 6:10)

Dear Lord, in a world that defines strength in so many ways, I thank you that my husband draws his strength from you. I praise you that my husband understands that real strength is displayed through the fruit of the Spirit. I thank you that my husband is loving. I thank you that he is peaceful and patient. I declare and decree that my husband is kind, gentle, good, faithful, and operates with self-control. Lord, remind him that his strength comes from your power and might, not by his might, not by his own power, but by Your Spirit. I pray he stands in certainty because of his union with you, knowing that nothing can separate him from your love.

In the name of Jesus, I pray, Amen.

July 17

"I have not departed from the commandment of His lips;
I have kept the words of His mouth more than my neces-
sary food." (Job 23:12)

Dear Lord, today I declare and decree that my husband's food is to do your will. I thank you that he keeps the words of your mouth dear to his heart. Thank you that he has chosen to live for you and has not strayed away from your commands. Thank you for a husband that takes your word seriously, not just being a hearer of the word, but a doer. Heavenly Father, I thank you for the conviction my husband has in keeping your words and treasures them more than natural food. Continue to lead and guide him to seek you above all else and make his spirit sensitive to your leading in prayer and fasting.

In the name of Jesus, I pray, Amen.

July 18

"I remember the days of old; I meditate on all Your works; I muse on the work of Your hands."
(Psalm 143: 5)

Dear Lord, thank you for giving my husband hope. I pray that you would let him see you in the ordinary things in this world. Let him sense you in his interactions. I pray he be in awe of you when he looks upon the works of your hands. I pray that your Spirit would lead him to be quiet and to recognize and relish all the beauty in the things you have made. I pray that he would find contentment in you and that you would fill his soul (his mind, will, and emotions) with your presence. I pray he finds beauty in your creation.

In the name of Jesus, I pray, Amen.

July 19

"Then he answered and spake unto me, saying, This is the word of Jehovah unto Zerubbabel, saying, Not by might, nor by power, but by my Spirit, saith Jehovah of hosts."
(Zechariah 4:6)

Dear Lord, I thank you for what you are doing in my husband's life today. I declare and decree that my husband is a man of godly strength. I pray he understands that anything he does, is not because of his own strength, wit, or merit but it is because your Spirit leads him and favors him. Holy Spirit, continue to lead him in the way that he should go. And if he does not know you, I pray right now that you would become known in his life. Show him you. Show him, your Majesty. Lead his heart to ask, "What must I do to be saved?" Save his soul, dear Lord.

In the name of Jesus, I pray, Amen.

July 20

*"Jesus said to him, "I am the [only] Way [to God] and the [real] Truth and the [real] Life; no one comes to the Father but through Me." **(John 14:6)***

Dear Lord, thank you for saving my husband. Thank you that he has received the revelation that you are the Way, the Truth, and the Life. Thank you that he has come through you, Jesus, to get to the Father. I pray that my husband would have a heart that is open to the leading of your Spirit, and that he would be willing to follow wherever you lead him. I pray that he would seek to know you more intimately, and that he would experience the peace and joy that come from a life fully surrendered to you. May he point others toward the truth and hope, that can only be found in Christ.

In the name of Jesus, I pray, Amen.

July 21

"For this very reason, applying your diligence [to the divine promises, make every effort] in [exercising] your faith to, develop moral excellence, and in moral excellence, knowledge (insight, understanding),"

(2 Peter 1:5)

Dear Lord, thank you for showing us a more excellent way. I declare and decree that my husband is a man of integrity and diligence. Help him, Lord, to continue to develop that integrity in ministry, with business, with people, and with our family. Please grant him the virtues of faith, goodness, knowledge, self-control, perseverance, godliness, brotherly kindness, and love. And Lord, give him the wisdom to know how to apply these virtues in his daily life. I also pray that he would experience and receive your grace and mercy when he falls short and that he would be quick to repent and seek your forgiveness. I pray he continues to shine the light of your love and truth wherever he goes.

In the name of Jesus, I pray, Amen.

July 22

"and in your knowledge self-control; and in your self-control patience; and in your patience godliness; and in your godliness brotherly kindness; and in your brotherly kindness love." (2 Peter 1:6-7)

Dear Lord, to add to my prayer from yesterday I pray that his "self-control muscle" continues to be developed from day to day. Remind him that there is no temptation that comes to him, that is not common to man, and that you have already provided a way of escape. I declare and decree that my husband is a man of patience. I pray he be steadfast in his faith and not waver in difficult times, but instead persevere with godly character. Help him to pursue godliness, brotherly kindness, and love. I pray he grows in these qualities and not be ineffective in his spiritual journey. I pray that he may be a shining light to those around him, reflecting the fruit of the Spirit. Thank you, Lord, that he looks more and more like you each day.

In the name of Jesus, I pray, Amen.

233

July 23

"For as these qualities are yours and are increasing [in you as you grow toward spiritual maturity], they will keep you from being useless and unproductive in regard to the true knowledge and greater understanding of our Lord Jesus Christ." **(2 Peter 1:8)**

Dear Lord, I thank you that my husband possesses these qualities and that they are increasing. I declare and decree that my husband will continue to grow in the knowledge of Christ. Arrange divine appointments so that he acquires a greater understanding and appreciation of you. Thank you for giving him insight and wisdom concerning his future and identity in you. Open his eyes to more than what is in the natural. Give him the eyes of Christ. Remind him of who he is in Christ and the power of the resurrection that is present in his life.

In the name of Jesus, I pray, Amen.

July 24

"Uphold my steps in Your paths, that my footsteps may not slip. I have called upon You, for You will hear me, O God; incline Your ear to me, and hear my speech. Show Your marvelous lovingkindness by Your right hand, O You who save those who trust in You from those who rise up against them." (Psalm 17:5-7)

Dear Lord, I praise you and thank you that you hear my husband's prayers as he cries out to you for guidance and protection. I pray he finds refuge in you, and may you be his portion forever. I pray that you would set your gaze upon him and listen to his cry, for he trusts in you and seeks your face. Keep him as the apple of your eye and hide him in the shadow of your wings. Protect him from harm and guard him against those who are against him. I pray he continues to seek you with his whole heart, and I pray he finds strength and comfort in your unfailing love.

In the name of Jesus, I pray, Amen.

July 25

"Wherefore, brethren, give the more diligence to make your calling and election sure: for if ye do these things, ye shall never stumble:" **(2 Peter 1:10)**

Dear Lord, thank you for equipping my husband with the tools and insight needed to make his calling and election sure. I praise you for him being a man of integrity and a man of great diligence. Give him strength where he is weak and reassure him that he has everything he needs in you. I praise you that he does not stumble. Create in him a clean heart so that he can live a blameless life. Help him to know that it is attainable, because of the Holy Spirit which gives him the power. Thank you for the gift of his life, and for the eternal life that comes from knowing you.

In the name of Jesus, I pray, Amen.

July 26

"Call to Me and I will answer you, and tell you [and even show you] great and mighty things, [things which have been confined and hidden], which you do not know and understand and cannot distinguish." ***(Jeremiah 33:3)***

Dear Lord, first I want to thank you for the access I have to you. Your word says you will answer when I call. Thank you for that privilege! I call to you today, for my husband, and I ask that you reveal to him the wonderful things that you have in store for him. Show him the great and mighty things; things that have been confined and hidden. Lord, give him divine revelation and insight as he calls to you, and you answer. I pray he trusts in you and has faith that you will guide him on the path that you have set before him. I pray he finds comfort and hope in your promises, and I pray he continues to seek you with his whole heart. Thank you for your unending love and grace, and for the blessings that you have given to our family.

In the name of Jesus, I pray, Amen.

July 27

*"I know your works. See, I have set before you an open door, and no one can shut it; for you have a little strength, have kept My word, and have not denied My name." (**Revelation 3:8**)*

Dear Lord, I praise you for the brand-new mercies we see this morning! Great is your faithfulness towards us. Today I pray for my husband and ask that you open doors for him that no one can shut, and that you close doors that no one can open. I pray he has the faith to believe that you hold the key to his future and that you have a purpose for him. I pray that he would walk through the doors that you have opened for him with confidence and boldness, knowing that you are with him every step of the way. Thank you for your guidance and provision.

In the name of Jesus, I pray, Amen.

July 28

*"Religion that is pure and undefiled before God the Father is this: to visit orphans and widows in their affliction, and to keep oneself unstained from the world." (**James 1:27**)*

Dear Lord, I come to you today in prayer for my husband, and I pray that he may live a life that is pure and undefiled. Lord, give him a heart for those who are in need and show compassion to the less fortunate. Lead and guide him to keep himself from being polluted by the world. Keep him steadfast in his faith, so that he may be a positive influence on those around him. I pray that he may be an example of true faith, doing good works that are pure and undefiled before God. Thank you for his life and for your unending love and grace.

In the name of Jesus, I pray, Amen.

July 29

*"Be kind and compassionate to one another, forgiving
each other just as in Christ God forgave you."*
(Ephesians 4:32)

Dear Lord, I thank you for the gift of my husband. I
ask that you help him to be kind and compassionate to
those around him, forgiving others as you have forgiv-
en him. I pray he is quick to show mercy and grace,
and slow to anger, extending love and kindness to all
those he encounters. I pray he seeks to understand
others and put their needs before his own, just as you
have done for him. I pray that he is an example of your
forgiveness and that you bring healing and reconcilia-
tion to any broken relationships in his life. Help him
to display kindness, compassion, and forgiveness in
marriage, being a representation of your love for the
church.

In the name of Jesus, I pray, Amen.

July 30

"but you will receive power when the Holy Spirit has come upon you, and you shall be My witnesses both in Jerusalem and in all Judea, and Samaria, and as far as the remotest part of the earth." **(Acts 1:8)**

Dear Lord, thank you for the resurrection power that dwells and flows through my husband. Thank you for the active working of the Holy Spirit in his life. Empower him to be a witness for you, both in word and in deed. I pray he experiences your wonder-working power in every aspect of his life. Give him opportunities and the boldness to share his faith with those who need to hear the gospel. I pray he has the audacity to step out in faith, even when it is uncomfortable or challenging, knowing that you are with him every step of the way. I thank you for what you are doing in his life and pray that you continue to be God in his life all the days of his life.

In the name of Jesus, I pray, Amen.

July 31

"You are the salt of the earth..." **(Matthew 5:13a)**

Dear Lord, I thank you for a man that is the salt of the earth. I thank you that when my husband walks into the room the atmosphere shifts because he is full of you. I pray he brings a holy flavor to his environments at work, home, and in the community. Give him a newness and a zeal to be different and to be a preserver of truth and goodness. I ask that you give him the wisdom and discernment to know when and how to speak truth into the lives of others and to be a positive influence in whatever capacity he serves.

In the name of Jesus, I pray, Amen.

AUGUST

August 1

*"Coming to Him as to a living stone, rejected indeed by men, but chosen by God and precious, you also, as living stones, are being built up a spiritual house, a holy priesthood, to offer up spiritual sacrifices acceptable to God through Jesus Christ." (**Peter 2:4-5**)*

Dear Lord, I pray for my husband and ask that he may come to you as a living stone. Although he may have been rejected by people, he is chosen and precious in your sight. I pray he builds his life on the firm foundation of your love and grace, and he finds his identity in you. Help him to build up his spiritual house, to be a holy priesthood, and to offer spiritual sacrifices that are pleasing to you. I pray that he may have a heart that is fully devoted to you and that he may walk in the fullness of your calling for his life. I pray he is a strong and steady presence in our family, pointing us toward you. Lord, I pray he be a shining light in the world, reflecting your love and goodness to all those he encounters, even today.

In the name of Jesus, I pray, Amen.

August 2

*"Surely I have calmed and quieted my soul, like a weaned child with his mother; like a weaned child is my soul within me." **(Psalm 131:2)***

Dear Lord, I pray for my husband and ask that he find rest and peace in you, just as the psalmist. I pray he trusts in you with all his heart and lean not on his own understanding. Help him to find contentment in the knowledge that you are in control of all things, and that he can place his worries and fears in your hands. I pray he rests in your presence and find comfort in your love, knowing that you are with him always. I pray that he may grow in his faith and that he may have a heart that is fully devoted to you. Thank you for your love, mercy, and grace given to him as he continues to grow in you.

In the name of Jesus, I pray, Amen.

August 3

*"You make known to me the path of life; you will fill me with joy in your presence, with eternal pleasures at your right hand." (**Psalm 16:11**)*

Dear Lord, I thank you for a husband that seeks you to know the path for his life. The world offers many things, but none lead to the path you have made for him. Lord, help him to stay on the path you created for him. Help me to provide love, joy, grace, and support with his pursuit. I ask that you bless him and keep him safe all the days of his life, always guiding him along the path of righteousness. I pray he experiences the joy and fullness of life that comes from being in your presence and finds true contentment in your loving embrace.

In the name of Jesus, I pray, Amen.

August 4

"Honor the Lord with your wealth and with the first fruits of all your produce; then your barns will be filled with plenty, and your vats will be bursting with wine."
(Proverbs 3:9-10)

Dear Lord, I thank you for a husband that honors you in every area of his life. I pray that my husband will understand the importance of honoring you with his finances and that you would bless the works of his hands. I pray he finds joy in giving to others and experiences the abundance that comes from trusting in you. Lord, guide him as he makes decisions about money, and help him to manage his resources with wisdom and generosity. May our family always put you first in everything and may your provision for us be overflowing.

In the name of Jesus, I pray, Amen.

August 5

"For where your treasure is, there your heart will be also." (Matthew 6:21)

Dear Lord, thank you that my husband keeps his heart and mind fixed on things that are truly valuable and that bring him closer to you. Help him to live a life that honors and glorifies you. I pray he will seek first your kingdom and your righteousness and trust that all other things will be added unto him. May his love for you and his desire to serve you be where his treasure is, not money, clout, fame, accolades, or attention. I pray that he will always be mindful of the true treasures that you have in store for him both in this life and the next.

In the name of Jesus, I pray, Amen.

August 6

*"Take care, and be on your guard against all covetousness, for one's life does not consist in the abundance of his possessions." (**Luke 12:15**)*

Dear Lord, I come before you today to lift my husband in prayer, knowing that he is constantly bombarded by the pressures and demands of this world. I pray that he would find his satisfaction in you alone. Teach him to be content whatever the circumstance and give him a heart that is full of joy. I pray he always be reminded of your love and provision for him. Your word prompts us to be on guard and that life does not consist of an abundance of possessions. I ask that you help my husband to hold this truth close to his heart. Help him to focus on the things that truly matter, and above all else to seek your kingdom.

In the name of Jesus, I pray, Amen.

August 7

*"The rich rules over the poor, and the borrower is the slave of the lender." (**Proverbs 22:7**)*

Dear God, I thank you for the financial freedom that is available because of you! I pray that you would break the chains of debt that hold my husband captive, and give him the strength and wisdom to overcome generational curses of poverty, in the name of Jesus. I bind and cancel the generational curse of poverty over our lives right now in the Name of Jesus! Lord release divine provision and elevation in our lives today! Help him to seek your wisdom and guidance in financial endeavors and to trust in your provision, knowing that you are the one who can truly set him free. Help him to be a good steward of the resources you have given him. I ask that your favor rest upon him as he seeks to honor you with his finances. May he find his security and hope in you alone, and may his trust in you grow stronger with each passing day.

In the name of Jesus, I pray, Amen.

August 8

*"And just as you want men to do to you, you also do to them likewise." (**Luke 6:31**)*

Dear Lord, I am thankful today for a husband who is a man of integrity. Thank you that his integrity is defined by the way he treats those who can do nothing for him. He is compassionate, kind, and attentive to the needs of others, treating people the way that he wants to be treated and the way you would treat people. Thank you that he chooses to do what is right and he takes pleasure in doing the right thing when no one is looking. Thank you, Lord, for my mighty man of God!

In the name of Jesus, I pray, Amen.

August 9

"For the word of God is alive and active. Sharper than any double-edged sword, it penetrates even to dividing soul and spirit, joints and marrow; it judges the thoughts and attitudes of the heart." **(Hebrews 4:12)**

Dear Lord, I thank you for your word and that it is alive and active in my husband's life. I pray that when he reads Your Word, it comes alive in his heart. Judge the thoughts and attitudes of his heart. Let the Word penetrate it. Speak to him where I cannot. I trust you with his heart. May your word be a source of comfort and encouragement for him, and may it guide him in all his decisions and actions. Let it divide his soul and spirit; joints and marrow. Let it fine tune him on the inside. I pray that he would be filled with a hunger for your word, and that he would be diligent in studying and applying it to his life. May he be transformed by the renewing of his mind, and may he become a man after your own heart.

In the name of Jesus, I pray, Amen.

August 10

"And my God will supply every need of yours according to his riches in glory in Christ Jesus."
(Philippians 4:19)

Dear Lord, I come before you today to lift my husband in prayer, knowing that he has needs that only you can provide. I pray that you would meet my husband at his point of need and provide for him in ways that he cannot even imagine. I pray he experiences your abundant provision and feel your loving care for him today. Help him to trust in your faithfulness and to rest in the assurance that you will always be there for him. Show him, Lord, that your love is not based on his performance, but is simply because you chose to love him. I pray he continues to find joy and peace in your presence and be filled with gratitude for all that you do in his life. I declare and decree that the blessings of the Lord are overtaking him in every area of his life.

In the name of Jesus, I pray, Amen.

August 11

*"My fellow believers, do not practice your faith in our glorious Lord Jesus Christ with an attitude of partiality [toward people—show no favoritism, no prejudice, no snobbery]." **(James 2:1)***

Dear Lord, I praise you for a husband that shows no partiality but chooses to love his neighbors as himself. I pray that you would give my husband the eyes of Christ and help him to see others as you see them, and to love them with the same love that you have shown him. I pray he continues to walk with integrity, treating everyone with respect and kindness, regardless of their background or social status. Help him to be a true friend to those in need, and to be a shining light in this dark, dark world.

In the name of Jesus, I pray, Amen.

August 12

*"Therefore my heart was glad and my tongue rejoiced;
my body also will live in hope," (**Acts 2:26**)*

Dear Lord, I thank you for bringing gladness to the heart of my husband. I pray his speech is fruitful and positive. Thank you that his conversations are edifying, blessing others, and giving you praise. Teach him not to focus on circumstances and when his heart is sad, dear Lord, overwhelm and fill his heart with your divine love. joy, and hope.

In the name of Jesus, I pray, Amen.

August 13

"and live in love, just as Christ also loved us and gave himself for us, a sacrificial and fragrant offering to God."
(Ephesians 5:2)

Dear Lord, as my husband goes about his day today, I pray that he would be filled with your love and that he would demonstrate that love to others in every aspect of his life. Help him to be patient, kind, and compassionate towards those around him, and to extend grace and forgiveness to those who have wronged him. I pray he be a living testimony of your love, and most importantly, may his actions point others to the sacrificial love of Christ. I thank you, God, that you so loved the world that you gave your only begotten son, Jesus - because of love. God, you are love. And because your Spirit lives in my husband, he is love. Gently remind his spirit today of the love you have for him and the love he has the privilege to share.

In the name of Jesus, I pray, Amen.

August 14

"Blessed is the man who endures temptation; for when he has been approved, he will receive the crown of life which the Lord has promised to those who love Him."
(James 1:12)

Dear Lord, I lift my husband to you in prayer. Thank you, Lord, for the blessings attached to enduring temptation. Lord, I know that men face unique temptations that can be difficult to resist. I ask that you give my husband the strength to resist temptations and to persevere through trials. Remind him of the promise of the crown of life. Guide him in your ways and lead him on the path of righteousness. Cancel any plans Satan has orchestrated to distract and deter him from carrying out your will for him today. I pray that you would protect him from harm and keep him close to you always.

In the name of Jesus, I pray, Amen.

August 15

*"Precious treasure and oil are in a wise man's dwelling, but a foolish man devours it." (**Proverbs 21:20**)*

Dear Lord, thank you for being a good and gracious God. Lord, I pray that my husband has the gift of wisdom so that he will make intelligent decisions and store up treasures that have eternal value. I pray he is not swayed by the world's values but instead seeks after your truth and righteousness. Give him discernment to recognize the choices that will lead to a fruitful and fulfilling life, avoiding those that would lead him astray. Help him to trust in you and to seek your guidance in all things.

In the name of Jesus, I pray, Amen.

August 16

"For the love of money is a root of all kinds of evils. It is through this craving that some have wandered away from the faith and pierced themselves with many pangs." (1 Timothy 6:10)

Dear Lord, today I pray for my husband to be consistent in trusting your provision. I pray that you would guard my husband's heart against the love of money and that he would find contentment in you alone. Help him to trust in your divine provision and to resist the temptations that come with wealth and material possessions. I pray that you would grant him wisdom in managing his finances as you enlarge his territory. Place in him the desire to use his resources to bless others and advance your kingdom. I pray he always put his faith in you and not in the things of this world. Strengthen his faith and help him to remain steadfast in your love.

In the name of Jesus, I pray, Amen.

August 17

*"You shall remember the Lord your God, for it is he who gives you power to get wealth, that he may confirm his covenant that he swore to your fathers, as it is this day." (**Deuteronomy 8:18**)*

Dear Lord, I pray that my husband would always remember that it is you who has given him the ability to succeed and prosper in his endeavors. I pray he never forgets to give you the glory for all that he has accomplished and to recognize that all good things come from you. Help him to use his talents and resources for your glory and to advance your kingdom. I pray he always acknowledges your hand in his life and trusts in your provision. I pray that you would bless him with an abundance of wisdom, discernment, and divine connections.

In the name of Jesus, I pray, Amen.

August 18

"One gives freely, yet grows all the richer; another with-holds what he should give, and only suffers want. Whoev-er brings blessing will be enriched, and one who waters will himself be watered."
(Proverbs 11:24-25)

Dear Lord, I pray that you would bless my husband with a generous heart and a spirit of giving. I pray he understands that true prosperity comes not from self-ish accumulation, but from giving generously to oth-ers. Help him to be a source of refreshment to those around him, and to always be willing to give of his time, talents, and resources to those in need. I pray he never holds back out of fear or selfishness but trusts in your leading and give freely as you direct him. Bless him abundantly as he seeks to bless others and use him as an instrument of your love and generosity in this world.

In the name of Jesus, I pray, Amen.

August 19

"No one can serve two masters; for either he will hate the one and love the other, or else he will be loyal to the one and despise the other. You cannot serve God and mammon." (Matthew 6:24)

Dear Lord, I come to you in prayer with a heart of gratitude for my dear husband. Today I pray he would always choose to serve you as his master, find joy and fulfillment in serving you, and remain loyal to you in all things. Help him to love you with all his heart, soul, mind, and strength. Open his eyes to detect the tricks of the enemy that come to trap him. I pray he is not swayed by the temptations of this world, but instead, walks confidently in the spirit. May he trust in your provision and seek after your will for his life. May his love for you be evident in all his pursuits, as he continues to serve you with gladness in his heart. Strengthen his faith and guide him in all his ways.

In the name of Jesus, I pray, Amen.

August 20

"Each one must give as he has decided in his heart, not reluctantly or under compulsion, for God loves a cheerful giver." (2 Corinthians 9:7)

Dear Lord, I thank you that my husband has a cheerful heart and is willing to give generously to others. Thank you that he is not an impulsive spender or a reluctant giver. I praise you that he has found joy in giving. May he be a conduit of your love and provision to those around him. I pray that he does not operate from a clenched fist. Help him to be a wise steward to what you have entrusted to him, and to always seek your guidance in managing his finances. May he not give out of obligation or pressure, but out of a genuine desire to bless others. May his giving be a reflection of your love and generosity, and may it bring glory to your Name. Strengthen his faith and guide him in all of his ways.

In the name of Jesus, I pray, Amen.

August 21

"Do not withhold good from those to whom it is due,
When it is in the power of your hand to do so."
(Proverbs 3:27)

Dear Lord, I thank you that my husband is an excellent spiritual leader. He does not abuse power, but he leads with humility and divine insight. I pray he is sensitive to the needs of those around him. Give him a spirit of compassion and kindness, a heart willing to do good for others, and to lend a helping hand. Make him to be a source of encouragement and support to those who are struggling. Lead and guide him as he needs, so that his kindness is not mistaken for weakness. I pray he reflects your love and goodness in this world, and may his actions bring honor and glory to your Name. Continue to strengthen his faith and direct him in all his ways.

In the name of Jesus, I pray, Amen.

August 22

*"He will not allow your foot to slip; He who keeps you will not slumber." **(Psalm 121:3)***

Dear Lord, thank you for divine protection and for the angels you have dispatched to watch over us day after day. I pray that you would carry my husband in the palm of your hands. Though the road may get tough, and he may become weary, remind him not to get weary in well-doing because of the reaping if he faints not. Thank you for caring so much for my husband that you will not allow his foot to slip. Thank you for being right there for him. I pray he rests in the comfort of knowing - He who keeps us will not slumber. Thank you for keeping him. So, Lord, when things catch him by surprise, remind him that it had to come by you first and that you have his best interest at heart.

In the name of Jesus, I pray, Amen.

August 23

*"Now this I know: The LORD gives victory to his anoint-
ed. He answers him from his heavenly sanctuary with the
victorious power of his right hand."*
(Psalm 20:6)

Dear Lord, I thank you that in the name of Jesus, we
have the victory! Thank you for answering us from
your heavenly sanctuary and loving us enough to
come to see about us. I pray that my husband would
trust in you and know that you are the giver of victory.
I pray he seeks your face daily and find strength and
guidance in Your Word. May your anointing rest upon
him and give him the courage and wisdom he needs to
face every challenge that comes his way. I pray he
knows that you are always with him and that you will
answer him when he calls out to you. May your victorious power be at work in his life, and I pray he experiences your goodness and grace in all that he does.
Bless him abundantly and guide him in all his ways.

In the name of Jesus, I pray, Amen.

August 24

"They all joined together constantly in prayer, along with the women and Mary the mother of Jesus, and with his brothers." (Acts 1:14)

Dear Lord, today I pray that my husband would be a man of prayer, constantly seeking your face and communing with you. May we be surrounded by a community of believers who will support him in prayer and encourage him in his faith. Help him to draw strength and wisdom from your Word, and to seek your guidance in all that he does. May his heart be filled with love and compassion for those around him, and I pray he be a source of light and hope in our home and to others. Bless him with good health, peace of mind, and prosperity, and I pray he uses all that you have given him for your glory. Strengthen his prayer life and help us to make prayer and communion with you a common practice in our home and in our marriage.

In the name of Jesus, I pray, Amen.

August 25

*"Therefore put away all filthiness and rampant wicked-ness and receive with meekness the implanted word, which is able to save your souls." **(James 1:21)***

Dear God, your teachings tell us that the heart can be deceitful. Today, I ask for your help to mend and cultivate my husband's heart. I pray that his heart becomes receptive to Your Word, removing anything that is not pleasing to you. I pray against any wicked-ness or impurities that try to harm our marriage. Instead, I declare that my husband and I always operate in love and purity. I pray that he pursues holiness and righteousness with diligence and is quick to confess and repent of any wrongdoing. Please help him to humbly accept Your Word and let it take root in his heart, bringing forth the fruit of the Spirit. I pray that he lives a life of integrity and character that is pleasing to you and inspiring to others.

In the name of Jesus, I pray, Amen.

August 26

"Do not merely listen to the word, and so deceive your-selves. Do what it says." (James 1:22)

Dear Lord, I thank you for the access we have to your word. Thank you that your word is a lamp to our feet and that it lights our paths. Thank you for connecting us to a word-based church that teaches the truth of your word and challenges us to be better every day. I pray that my husband would embody the word. I pray that you would assist him in grasping the importance of not merely listening to the word, but doing what it says. Block any deceptive tactics the enemy has established to make him believe anything other than the importance of living out the word in his everyday life. Empower him to walk out the word with fear and reverence for you. Strengthen him where he is weak. Remind him that he doesn't have to walk alone.

In the name of Jesus, I pray, Amen.

August 27

*"If anyone thinks he is religious and does not bridle his tongue but deceives his heart, this person's religion is worthless." **(James 1:26)***

Dear Lord, I pray my husband will always be mindful of the words he speaks, and that he will guard his tongue from speaking any harmful or unkind words. As James 1:26 reminds us, those who consider themselves religious and yet do not keep a tight rein on their tongues deceive themselves, and their religion is worthless. Lord, I pray that my husband will not fall into this trap, but rather, use his words to build others up and bring glory to your name. Help him to speak truth with love, and to be a shining example of your grace and mercy in our marriage and in all that he says and does.

In the name of Jesus, I pray, Amen.

August 28

*"For thus said the Lord Jehovah, the Holy One of Israel, In returning and rest shall ye be saved; in quietness and in confidence shall be your strength." **(Isaiah 30:15)***

Dear Lord, I pray that my husband will find rest in you and turn to you in repentance. Help him to trust in your strength and find peace in the quietness of his heart. I pray he finds comfort in knowing that you are with him always, guiding him along the path of righteousness. I pray he also finds rest and refreshment in his daily life, knowing that you are always there to comfort him and give him the strength to face whatever challenges come his way. Give him confidence and teach him to be comfortable in the quiet moments so that he can draw from your strength. I pray he always trusts in you and relies on your wisdom and guidance.

In the name of Jesus, I pray, Amen.

August 29

"Anyone who listens to the word but does not do what it says is like someone who looks at his face in a mirror and, after looking at himself, goes away and immediately forgets what he looks like." (James 1:23-24)

Dear Lord, I thank you that my husband is confident in who he is in you. I thank you that he knows what you say about him and that he rests in that. Lord, I pray that my husband will not only hear your word, but he will also put it into practice in his daily life. I pray he leans on your guidance and wisdom in all that he does, and he follows your commandments with a willing and obedient heart. Help him to remember that the true measure of his faith is not in what he hears, or what he says, but in what he does. May his actions always reflect his love and devotion to you, and I pray he continues to operate in the fruit of the Spirit.

In the name of Jesus, I pray, Amen.

August 30

*"But whoever looks intently into the perfect law that gives freedom, and continues in it—not forgetting what they have heard, but doing it—they will be blessed in what they do." (**James 1:25**)*

Dear Lord, I praise you for the promises in your word. There are so many blessings attached to obedience. I pray that my husband is a man of obedience and that you continue to mature him in the faith. I pray he looks intently at the perfect law that gives freedom and continues in it. May he find the freedom your word speaks about and relish in it. Let him not forget what he has heard but hold it in his heart with good intentions to obey it. Bless his going out and his coming in. Bless his mind, his body, and his spirit. Purify his soul.

In the name of Jesus, I pray, Amen.

August 31

"Blessed are the merciful: for they shall obtain mercy."
(Matthew 5:7)

Dear Lord, I praise you for being a merciful God. I pray that you will pour out your mercy upon my husband and that he will also show mercy to those around him. Continue to develop in him compassion and kind-heartedness. I pray that he will show love and forgiveness to those who have wronged him. I pray he will seek to understand others and be a source of comfort and support to those who are hurting. I pray that he will be a living example of your mercy and that he will inspire others. I pray he is blessed with an abundance of your love and grace, and that his life be a testament to your goodness and faithfulness.

In the name of Jesus, I pray, Amen.

SEPTEMBER

September 1

"Where there is no [wise, intelligent] guidance, the people fall [and go off course like a ship without a helm], But in the abundance of [wise and godly] counselors there is victory." **(Proverbs 11:14)**

Dear Lord, I pray that my husband will seek wise counsel from others as he navigates the challenges of life. Help him to surround himself with people who will encourage and support him, and who will offer him sound advice when he needs it. I pray he also be a source of guidance and support to those around him, sharing his wisdom and insight with others. I pray that he will never feel alone or lost, but that he will always be surrounded by a strong network of friends and loved ones. May his relationships be marked by trust, respect, and mutual support. I pray he always finds victory and success through the counsel of godly mentors.

In the name of Jesus, I pray, Amen.

September 2

"Great is our Lord, and mighty in power; His under-standing is infinite." **(Psalm 147:5)**

Dear Lord, you are great and mighty in power! Your understanding is infinite. No one can contend with you. You are our great Defender! Lord, I ask that you remind my husband of your greatness and your strength. I pray that my husband will always trust in your infinite understanding and strength and that he will find comfort and hope in your promises. Your power is beyond measure, and your wisdom is unfathomable. You are the Almighty God, and nothing is impossible for you. May my husband be filled with awe and wonder at the magnificence of your being, and I pray he is strengthened and encouraged by you. Thank you for your faithfulness and your constant presence. Thank you, Lord, for the gift of my husband, and for your never-ending love and faithfulness.

In the name of Jesus, I pray, Amen.

September 3

*"Do you not know? Have you not heard? The LORD is the everlasting God, the Creator of the ends of the earth. He will not grow tired or weary, and his understanding no one can fathom." (**Isaiah 40:28**)*

Dear Lord, you are the Creator of everything! You are the everlasting God and I bless your Holy Name. How majestic are you, Lord! We get tired and weary, but Lord, you never do. I pray that you will reveal to my husband your everlasting nature and your infinite power. I pray that my husband will find strength and hope in the truth that you never grow weary and that we cannot begin to fathom your understanding. I pray that he will learn to trust in your unchanging nature. I pray he is filled with the peace and confidence that comes from knowing that you are in control of all things. I thank you for your faithfulness and for the privilege of being able to pray for my husband.

In the name of Jesus, I pray, Amen.

September 4

"Those whom I love, I rebuke and discipline; therefore be zealous and repent." (Revelation 3:19)

Dear Lord, today I ask that you work in the heart and mind of my husband. You discipline and chasten those whom you love, so I pray that my husband will recognize and receive your loving correction and humbly heed your guidance, surrendering his life to your purpose. Help him to grow in his relationship and to become more like you in his thoughts, words, and actions. Give him the courage to face his weaknesses and shortcomings, and the strength to overcome them with the help of the Holy Spirit.

In the name of Jesus, I pray, Amen.

September 5

"Behold what manner of love the Father has bestowed on us, that we should be called children of God! Therefore the world does not know us, because it did not know Him
(1 John 3:1)

Dear Lord, I thank you for the incredible love you have for us, and the amazing privilege that we have to be called your children. I pray that you would reveal to my husband this level of love so that he may pause and reflect on its truth, and allow it to sink deep into his heart. May he be filled with gratitude and awe at the wonder of our adoption into God's family, and may he never take for granted the love and grace that has been poured out upon him. I pray that he is encouraged and strengthened by the knowledge that he belongs to you and nothing can separate him from your love. I pray that he lives each day with confidence and joy as your beloved son, reflecting your love to those around him.

In the name of Jesus, I pray, Amen.

September 6

*"Therefore my heart was glad and my tongue was over-joyed;" **(Acts 2:26)***

Dear Lord, I thank you that my husband has joy, and his heart is glad. I pray that you would continue to heal past wounds and hurts that he is not aware are there. Thank you for his speech that is overflowing with great joy. I declare and decree that when my husband speaks, those around him will be empowered and experience joy as well. Thank you for using him to bring gladness and joy into different atmospheres and to our home. My heart is delighted, because you chose my husband to spread cheer and gladness to those around him. Thank you, Father.

In the name of Jesus, I pray, Amen.

September 7

"But if you show partiality [prejudice, favoritism], you are committing sin and are convicted by the Law as offenders." (James 2:9)

Thank you for creating my husband in your image, which allows him to treat others with respect and dignity. I pray that he examines his heart and overcomes any biases or prejudices that he may have and that he sees others through your eyes of love and compassion. I pray for a husband who strives to treat everyone with kindness and fairness. May this begin in our home, and may he remember that by doing so, he is fulfilling the law of love that Jesus taught us to follow.

In the name of Jesus, I pray, Amen.

September 8

"My mouth shall tell of Your righteousness And Your salvation all the day, For I do not know their limits."
(Psalm 71:15)

Dear Lord, I come to you in prayer for my husband, asking that you bless him according to your steadfast love and faithfulness. I pray that my husband will be filled with a heart of gratitude and thanksgiving for all the ways you have shown love and mercy to him. I pray he is never ashamed or gets tired of proclaiming your goodness and your salvation to those around him. May his testimony be a powerful witness to your grace and love. I ask that you grant him the strength and courage to walk in your ways, and to trust in your unfailing love and faithfulness, even during trials and hardships. Thank you, Lord, for the gift of my husband, and for your never-ending love and grace.

In the name of Jesus, I pray, Amen.

September 9

*"I will go in the strength of the Lord GOD; I will make
mention of Your righteousness, of Yours only."*
(Psalm 71:16)

Dear Lord, I am grateful that our strength comes from
you. I ask that you remind my husband to rely on your
strength. Help him turn to you when he feels weak or
in need, knowing that you are his source of protection.
Let us not forget it is your righteousness that saves us,
not our efforts or achievements. I pray that my husband humbly acknowledges his need for you and is
grateful for your grace and mercy that sustain him
every day. May he always give thanks for your goodness and be a source of encouragement and hope to
those who may be struggling. Let him reflect your unconditional love and strength in all that he does. I pray
he goes forth in your power, giving you all the glory.

In the name of Jesus, I pray, Amen.

September 10

"For your Father knows the things you have need of before you ask Him." (Matthew 6:8)

Dear Lord, thank you for being an attentive God. Thank you for supplying our every need and being so interested in the affairs of our lives. Your word reminds us that you know the things we have need of before we even ask you. So, you know the very thing that my husband is needing today. Heavenly Father, I lift my husband up to you at this very moment. I pray that you will be God in his life today. Whatever he needs, I pray that you would supply. You are his father, and you have his best interests at heart. I trust you with his life. Thank you for intricately creating him and divinely placing him where you can carry out your will for his life. Bless my husband today.

In the name of Jesus, I pray, Amen.

September 11

"Consequently, he is able to save to the uttermost those who draw near to God through him, since he always lives to make intercession for them." **(Hebrews 7:25)**

Dear Lord, you are faithful, and your love is unrivaled. Thank you that you are making intercession for my husband. You know all his desires and all his needs. Today I pray my husband will experience a tugging in his heart and that he will desire to draw nearer to you. I am profoundly grateful to you for saving my husband. Thank you for grabbing him and never letting him go. You are the center of his joy and peace. Live in him and through him.

In the name of Jesus, I pray, Amen.

September 12

*"There is no other god like you, O LORD; you forgive the sins of your people who have survived. You do not stay angry forever, but you take pleasure in showing us your constant love." **(Micah 7:18)***

Dear Lord, your word declares, "There is no one like you!" I praise you for being the living God! Thank you for forgiving my husband's sins and the sins of his ancestors. Thank you for your grace, mercy, and love. According to scripture, you do not remain angry forever. I ask that you continue to extend your grace and forgiveness to my husband, washing his sins. You take pleasure in giving and showing your unceasing love. I pray my husband patterns his life after you, taking pleasure in showing his family grace and perpetual love. Thank you for being the example.

In the name of Jesus, I pray, Amen.

September 13

*"And suddenly there came from heaven a sound like a mighty rushing wind, and it filled the entire house where they were sitting." **(Acts 2:2)***

Dear Lord, just like you did on the day of Pentecost, I pray that a rushing, mighty wind would fill our home and rest on us. If we are living in different residences, I pray that You would fill my husband with the Holy Spirit and that he would begin to speak with different tongues as Your Spirit gives him the ability. Sweep through every room, shifting the atmosphere in our home(s). Lord, fill my husband and fill me with your glory. You are welcome to invade our spaces.

In the name of Jesus, I pray, Amen.

September 14

*"I have become a sign to many; you are my strong refuge." **(Psalm 71:7)***

Dear Lord, thank you for your protection and guidance, in the life of my husband. Thank you that his life is a testimony to your faithfulness and that your power and provision are evident to those around him. Despite any challenges he may face, I pray that my husband will find safety and security in you. Thank you for being a mighty God and a great Defender in every circumstance. You are the God who can be trusted and a strong refuge.

In the name of Jesus, I pray, Amen.

September 15

"Before they call I will answer; while they are still speaking I will hear." (Isaiah 65:24)

Dear Lord, you are an awesome God! I praise you for always being attentive to my husband's needs and already at work on his behalf before he even asks. I pray that you would encourage my husband's heart today. Give him comfort in knowing that you are always listening and always ready to respond to his prayers, even before he can fully articulate them. I pray that your Spirit reminds my husband to trust in your divine provision, praying with confidence, knowing that you are willing and able to supply his every need.

In the name of Jesus, I pray, Amen.

September 16

*"For you make me glad by your deeds, LORD; I sing for joy at what your hands have done." **(Psalm 92:4)***

Dear Lord, I pray that you would give my husband a new song. Allow the work of your hands to be a reminder of your awesomeness. I pray he will see how amazing you are God. Make his heart glad. Thank you for what you are doing and have done in his life. Make joy a resident in his soul. Give him a new perspective on life so that when he takes in everything around him, his response is to sing of your goodness. I pray he proclaims your goodness and your deeds in his life to those near and far. I pray he be a testament to your greatness.

In the name of Jesus, I pray, Amen.

September 17

"Now may the Lord of peace himself give you peace at all times and in every way. The Lord be with all of you."
(2 Thessalonians 3:16)

Dear Lord, thank you for being our Peace. Today I ask that you would be with my husband and grant him a deep and everlasting sense of your peace, even when the world around him feels chaotic and uncertain. I pray he rests in the knowledge that you are in control and that you are working all things together for his good. I also pray that you would protect his heart and mind from fear and anxiety. Help him to trust in your love and provision and to lean on you in every moment. Lord, I pray that you would strengthen his faith and fill him with hope.

In the name of Jesus, I pray, Amen.

September 18

"The LORD will vindicate me; your love, LORD, endures forever — do not abandon the works of your hands."
(Psalm 138:8)

Dear Lord, I thank you for your vindication and love that endures forever. I pray my husband finds peace in knowing that you vindicate him and that he would trust in your unfailing love. You, Lord, are his source of strength and comfort in every circumstance. I pray that my husband would have confidence in the plan and the purpose you have for his life. Order his steps, guiding him and giving him wisdom in all that he does.

In the name of Jesus, I pray, Amen.

September 19

"For judgment will be merciless to one who has shown no mercy; mercy triumphs over judgment." (James 2:13)

Dear Lord, today my prayer for my husband is that he always shows mercy to others, even in difficult situations where it may be easier to judge or condemn. I pray he understands that through showing mercy, he not only reflects the love and compassion of Christ, but also receives mercy from you. I pray he has the humility to recognize his own shortcomings and to extend grace and forgiveness to himself as well as others. May the triumph of mercy over judgment be evident in his words, actions, and interactions with those around him, and I pray he be blessed with peace, joy, and fulfillment in his life as a result.

In the name of Jesus, I pray, Amen.

September 20

*"I pray he turn our hearts to him, to walk in obedience to him and keep the commands, decrees and laws he gave our ancestors." **(1 Kings 8:58)***

Dear Lord, I come to you with a grateful heart for my husband. I pray that he would be blessed with a heart that is fully devoted to you, seeking after you in all areas of his life. I pray he has a heart that is open to the leading of the Holy Spirit and willing to follow your ways. I pray he have the wisdom and discernment to make good decisions and to prioritize his relationship with you above all else. I pray he be strengthened and encouraged by your holy presence and divine guidance, and may our marriage be a testimony of your goodness, love, and grace. I declare and decree that my husband is a blessing to those around him, using his gifts and talents to serve and minister to others.

In the name of Jesus, I pray, Amen.

September 21

*"But you, L*ORD*, are a shield around me, my glory, the One who lifts my head high." **(Psalm 3:3)***

Dear Lord, I thank you for being a shield around my husband, his glory, and the lifter of his head. Today I pray that you would cover him from hurt and harm; physical and mental. Ward off any attack the enemy has orchestrated to kill, steal, and destroy on today. Shine your light through him so that in every capacity he operates in today, your glory will shine through. Where his face is downtrodden and his heart may be heavy, lift his head, Lord. Encourage his heart and his mind in you. Give him confidence as he rests in the fact that your shield is all around him and nothing, by any means, can harm him.

In the name of Jesus, I pray, Amen.

September 22

*"Dear children, let us not love with words or speech but with actions and in truth. This is how we know that we belong to the truth and how we set our hearts at rest in his presence:" (**1 John 3:18-19**)*

Dear Lord, I thank you that my husband is a man that loves with his actions and in truth. Grant him the divine revelation of your love so that he can operate in it daily. We know that he belongs to the truth because You are the living Word, and You are Truth. I pray he sets his heart to seek truth and righteousness and I pray he seeks Your Presence all the days of his life. Thank you that the truth and righteousness that my husband rests in infiltrates our home, marriage, and family. Thank you for such a mighty man of Valor!

In the name of Jesus, I pray, Amen.

September 23

"In him and through faith in him we may approach God with freedom and confidence." (Ephesians 3:12)

Dear Lord, I praise you because in you and through faith in you, we can approach you with freedom and confidence! What a privilege to know you and to be your child! Today I pray that my husband would rest in that truth because he is your child! I pray that you would grant him the peace of God to be able to come to you with freedom and with confidence. Where the enemy would try to come in like a flood in his mind and give him a reason to believe that he cannot or should not come to you, I pray that you would raise a standard against him and allow Your Spirit to comfort and lead him right back to you. Thank you for the access we have to you! Thank you for giving my husband everything he needs.

In the name of Jesus, I pray, Amen.

September 24

*"For such a person ought not to think or expect that he will receive anything [at all] from the Lord, being a double-minded man, unstable and restless in all his ways [in everything he thinks, feels, or decides]." **(James 1:7-8)***

Dear Lord, I thank you for a stable-minded husband. I pray that you would ground him in his thinking, feelings, and decisions. Let him not waver with the wind, but be steadfast, immovable, and always abounding in the work of the Lord. Grant him unwavering faith in your ability to grant him wisdom and discernment. I pray he trusts in your goodness and seeks your guidance in all areas of his life. I pray he be steadfast in his faith, rooted and grounded in your love, and I pray he receives the wisdom he seeks from you, Lord. May his heart be filled with peace, and I pray he be empowered to lead his family with grace and humility.

In the name of Jesus, I pray, Amen.

September 25

"Vindicate me, LORD, for I have led a blameless life; I have trusted in the LORD and have not faltered."
(Psalm 26:1)

Dear Lord, you are a faithful Father. Thank You. I pray for my husband today that he may trust in the Lord with all his heart and seek to lead a blameless life before you. I pray he has the courage to stand firm in his faith and live according to your will, even when faced with difficulties and temptation. I pray he be filled with the peace and joy that come from walking in righteousness. God, I pray you would vindicate him, protect him, and guide him as he follows you wholeheartedly. I pray he continues to grow in his relationship with you, experiencing blessings and favor in every area of his life. God remove anything in his life or within his grasp that would keep him from growing in you.

In the name of Jesus, I pray, Amen.

September 26

"This is the day which the LORD hath made; we will rejoice and be glad in it." **(Psalm 118:24)**

Dear Lord, this is the day that You have made, and I will rejoice and be glad. Today I pray that my husband may wake up every morning with a heart full of gratitude for the new day that you have given him. I pray he recognizes each day as a precious gift from above and live it to the fullest, with joy, purpose, and passion. I pray he finds joy and contentment in the simple things of life, and I pray he experiences your presence and blessings in all his interactions today. I pray that he would be filled with hope and optimism, even during difficult times, and that you would divinely strengthen him to overcome any challenges that come his way. I pray he always remembers that he is loved by you and that he has a purpose and a destiny in you.

In the name of Jesus, I pray, Amen.

September 27

"Let integrity and uprightness preserve me; for I wait on thee." (Psalm 25:21)

Dear Lord, today I pray for my husband's integrity and uprightness in all aspects of his life. May he understand the importance of living an honest, transparent, and authentic life and be committed to walking in righteousness and uprightness before you and others. I pray that he resists the temptation to compromise his values or character for personal gain and always does what is right, even if it is difficult. May his commitment to integrity be a shield of protection, guarding him against the enemy's attacks and allowing him to experience your blessings and favor. May his hope and trust be firmly rooted in you, and may he be empowered by the Holy Spirit to live a life of integrity and honor, that glorifies you, and blesses those around him.

In the name of Jesus, I pray, Amen.

September 28

"But may all who search for you be filled with joy and gladness in you. May those who love your salvation repeatedly shout, 'The LORD is great!'" **(Psalm 40:16)**

Dear Lord, you are great and greatly to be praised. Praise your holy Name! Lord, I pray my husband will seek you with all his heart finding joy and gladness in you. Let him not look to man or another woman to supply his need, but only look to you. I pray he be filled with gratitude for all that you have done for him, and he will be a living testimony to your greatness and faithfulness. I pray that my husband would experience the abundant life that comes from walking in close fellowship with you. May his heart be filled with a deep sense of awe and reverence for You, God, and I pray he be inspired to live a life that honors and glorifies you in all that he does. Mature his love for you, inspiring our family.

In the name of Jesus, I pray, Amen.

September 29

"And I am praying that you will put into action the generosity that comes from your faith as you understand and experience all the good things we have in Christ."
(Philemon 1:6)

Dear Lord, thank you for my husband, who is a faithful and generous man. I pray his partnership with other believers in the faith are fruitful and effective in deepening his understanding of every good thing. Surround him with a community of believers who encourage and support his walk with you and encourage growth in faith and knowledge. I pray he would be open to learning from others, sharing his experiences, and contributing to the body of Christ. May his faith be strengthened, his love for you and others deepened, and his witness for Christ be a shining light in this dark world. May his partnership with other believers be a source of joy and encouragement, and may it bear much fruit in the kingdom of God.

In the name of Jesus, I pray, Amen.

September 30

"If, however, you are [really] fulfilling the royal law according to the Scripture, "You shall love your neighbor as yourself [that is, if you have an unselfish concern for others and do things for their benefit]" you are doing well."
(James 2:8)

Dear Lord, I praise you for my husband's growth in you. Thank you for pouring your love on him and teaching him what it means to love his neighbor as himself. Fill his heart full of love for others, giving him the desire to treat others with the same kindness, compassion, and respect he wants for himself. I pray he has a spirit of generosity and is willing to help others and meet their needs, like the good Samaritan. Empower him through the Holy Spirit to love others as Christ loved us, and may his life be a living example of what it means to follow Christ.

In the name of Jesus, I pray, Amen.

OCTOBER

October 1

"I am the Alpha and the Omega," says the Lord God, "who is and who was and who is to come, the Almighty."
(Revelation 1:8)

Dear Lord, thank you for being the Alpha and the Omega, the beginning and the end and everything in between. You are the author and finisher of our faith and I trust you with my life and my husband's life. Lord, I pray that my husband will recognize and embrace your sovereignty and power in his life. May he find comfort and security in the fact that you are always present, providing for him and guiding him through all of life's ups and downs. I pray that he will be strengthened and encouraged by your power and presence in his life. May he be inspired to live a life that honors and glorifies you in all that he does. May my dear husband trust in your promises and rest in your love, knowing that you are faithful and true.

In the name of Jesus, I pray, Amen.

October 2

"Nations will come to your light, and kings to the bright-ness of your dawn." (Isaiah 60:3)

Dear Lord, I am grateful for my husband, and I pray that you guide him in all he does. Allow him to be a source of hope and inspiration to those around him, drawing them closer to you through his actions and words. Please bless him with good health, happiness, and success in all aspects of his life. May he find joy and fulfillment in his work, relationships, and hob-bies, and may he always feel loved and appreciated. Thank you for the gift of my husband and for the way your light shines through him, drawing others to you.

In the name of Jesus, I pray, Amen.

October 3

*"But the LORD's plans stand firm forever; his intentions can never be shaken." **(Psalm 33:11)***

Dear Lord, order the steps of my husband, leading him down the path of righteousness. I pray he always trusts in your plans and purposes for his life, and I pray he finds strength and peace in knowing that you are in control and that your intentions can never be shaken. Bless him with wisdom, courage, and discernment as he faces the challenges of each day, and I pray he always seeks your will in all that he does. Thank you for the gift of my husband, and may your grace and love be evident in our marriage each day.

In the name of Jesus, I pray, Amen.

October 4

*"I will bless the LORD who guides me; even at night my heart instructs me." **(Psalm 16:7)***

Dear Lord, I bless you today. You are so deserving of all the glory and honor. I come before you, lifting my husband up to you. I pray that my husband will always seek your guidance and follow your ways. Help him to trust in you and find refuge in your presence, even when it's the midnight season in his life. May he never be swayed by the temptations of this world, but instead, be rooted in your love and filled with your joy. Give him the strength to bless you regardless of the circumstance. May he always have a heart of gratitude and praise, knowing that you are the source of all the blessings in his life. I pray that he will walk in your path and experience the fullness of joy and blessings that follow obedience.

In the name of Jesus, I pray, Amen.

October 5

"for the LORD is your security. He will keep your foot from being caught in a trap." **(Proverbs 3:26)**

Dear God, I am grateful for the security you provide. Your watchful eye is always upon us, even when we wander. Thank you for protecting us and keeping us from harm's way. I pray for my husband today, asking that you hold him in the palm of your hand. Sometimes, we make choices that have unintended consequences. Despite any missteps he may have taken, I am thankful that you have kept him safe. You have shielded us from traps that would have otherwise ensnared us. I am grateful for your unwavering love and guidance. Please continue to lead my husband as he leads our family. Thank you, God.

In the name of Jesus, I pray, Amen.

October 6

"Ponder the path of your feet and let all your ways be established." (Proverbs 4:26)

Dear Lord, I thank you that my husband gives thought to where he decides to go and what he chooses to engage in. Thank you for a man of God that walks in the Spirit, and not after the desires of his flesh. I thank you that his mind is continuing to be made new and that he considers you first before making decisions. Establish his way in you and continue to surround him with godly men that can help sharpen him into the man of God you've called him to be. Thank you for divine connections in his life that lead to divine placement, growth and opportunities.

In the name of Jesus, I pray, Amen.

October 7

*"And God will generously provide all you need. Then you will always have everything you need, and plenty left over to share with others." **(2 Corinthians 9:8)***

Dear God, I am grateful to you for being our Provider, Jehovah Jireh. Your faithfulness and consistency are remarkable. Your promise to generously provide all we need is reassuring. I thank you for fulfilling that promise in my husband's life. Because of your generosity, he has more than enough. Please help him to recognize the abundance of blessings in his life. When he feels insufficient, remind him you have provided all things. You have even left him with some extra to share with others. You are an excellent Father, and I appreciate you. Thank you, God.

In the name of Jesus, I pray, Amen.

October 8

"I cry out to God Most High, to God who will fulfill his purpose for me." (Psalm 57:2)

Dear God, I sincerely ask that you fulfill your purpose in my husband's life. When he is confused, please help him trust your plan and have faith that you will guide him along the path you have set for him. Please give him the courage to step out in faith when he needs to and not question your leadership. I pray that he is filled with your wisdom and discernment so he can make the right decisions to stay on the right track. Help him always seek your will and surrender his desires to you. Thank you for the great plans you have in store for my husband, plans to prosper him and give him hope and a future. Thank you for hearing our cries and always being there. I trust you and know you will fulfill your purpose in his life and in our marriage.

In the name of Jesus, I pray, Amen.

October 9

*"He said, "If you will listen carefully to the voice of the
LORD your God and do what is right in his sight, obeying
his commands and keeping all his decrees, then I will not
make you suffer any of the diseases I sent on the Egyp-
tians; for I am the LORD who heals you."*
(Exodus 15:26)

Dear Lord, with you nothing is impossible. You are the
God who heals. Today, I am praying for my husband
to experience your healing power in every area of his
life. I pray his faith is activated and he can believe for
himself that you are his healer. As he surrenders his
life to you, walking in obedience, restore his health
and renew his strength. I claim the promise that by
your stripes he is healed. There is no sickness or disease that can overtake him. He is strong, healthy, and
of a sound mind.

In the name of Jesus, I pray, Amen.

October 10

"Yes, I am the vine; you are the branches. Those who remain in me, and I in them, will produce much fruit. For apart from me you can do nothing." (John 15:5)

Dear Lord, I thank you for the opportunity to stay connected to you. I pray for my husband today and ask that you would give him the desire to remain in you, to abide in your love, and to bear fruit that glorifies your name. May your Holy Spirit work in and through him, so that he may reflect your love, grace, and mercy to those around him. Help him to trust in you and to lean on your strength when he doesn't know which way to turn. Lord, make him a producer of good fruit. Reveal to him the difference between good fruit and artificial fruit. Thank you for your unfailing love and your constant presence in his life. I give you all the honor and the glory, now and forevermore.

In the name of Jesus, I pray, Amen.

October 11

*"God showed how much he loved us by sending his one and only Son into the world so that we might have eternal life through him." **(1 John 4:9)***

Dear Lord, thank you for your love and your grace. I pray that my husband would experience the fullness of your love and that he would be rooted and grounded in your grace. I pray he continues to discover new things about you, resulting in him falling deeper in love with you. Help him to recognize your sacrifice made for him on the cross, responding with a heart of gratitude and obedience. I pray that your love always surrounds him and that you continue to fill him with your joy and peace. Thank you for the privilege of praying for my husband.

In the name of Jesus, I pray, Amen.

October 12

"God arms me with strength, and he makes my way perfect." (Psalm 18:32)

Dear Lord, I pray for my husband and ask that you be his rock, fortress, and deliverer. Arm him with your strength and power. Equip him with everything he needs to face the challenges of today and in his life. Give him the wisdom to make the right decisions. I pray he never be shaken or discouraged, knowing you are always with him. Help him to trust your direction and rely on your strength in all he does. Make his way perfect because he follows you. Thank you, Lord, for loving him.

In the name of Jesus, I pray, Amen.

October 13

"But he must ask [for wisdom] in faith, without doubting [God's willingness to help], for the one who doubts is like a billowing surge of the sea that is blown about and tossed by the wind." **(James 1:6)**

Dear God, I am grateful for your constant care and support of me and my husband. I am blessed to have a husband with a strong, unshakeable faith in you. I pray that he continues to trust in your promises believing you can do more than he could ever imagine. I pray he is not swayed by doubts or fears, and that he has the courage to ask for what he needs. Lord, let his faith inspire and uplift those around him. I am excited to witness all you have planned for his life.

In the name of Jesus, I pray, Amen.

October 14

"I will give thanks to you, O LORD, among the peoples; I will sing praises to you among the nations."
(Psalm 108:3)

Dear God, I want to express my immense gratitude and thankfulness for your blessings. Your kindness and mercy have been limitless, and I feel humbled by your generosity. Thank you for granting us the gift of life and the ability to breathe. Thank you for your unwavering love and the sacrifice of your Son, Jesus Christ, who died for our sins. I am also grateful for your constant guidance, wisdom, protection, and provision. Your presence has been a source of comfort and strength. I appreciate the wonderful people in our lives, their love, support, and the enrichment they have brought. Please help my husband to remember that these blessings are from you and to never take them for granted.

In the name of Jesus, I pray, Amen.

October 15

"For Scripture says to Pharaoh: "I raised you up for this very purpose, that I might display my power in you and that my name might be proclaimed in all the earth."
(Romans 9:17)

Dear Lord, I ask that you reveal your power through my husband. Make him a conduit of your authority, glorifying you on the earth. As he is making your name great, make his name great. Bless him with a promotion that does not come from the north, south, east, or west. I pray his reputation goes before him, speaking his name in rooms he has yet to enter. Place him before great men and women of influence. Thank you for the unexpected blessings from unspecified people and places.

In the name of Jesus, I pray, Amen.

October 16

*"I am the Lord your God, who brought you up out of
Egypt. Open wide your mouth and I will fill it."*
(Psalm 81:10)

Dear Lord, You are our God. You are our Deliverer!
Thank you for bringing us out of bondage. What an
awesome God you are! I ask you today to fill my husband's mouth with wisdom and grace. Direct him to
speak with diligence and integrity. Fill his mouth in
the boardroom, factory, classroom and in the field.
Fill his mouth in our home. Let his speech be edifying. Let it bring glory to you. I open my mouth wide so
that you can fill it. Fill it with your words. Let my
words be edifying to those around me, especially to
my husband. Teach me how to speak life to my husband. Continue to fill my mouth with more of you.

In the name of Jesus, I pray, Amen.

October 17

*"Then Jesus said, "Come to me, all of you who are weary
and carry heavy burdens, and I will give you rest."*
(Matthew 11:28)

Dear Lord, thank you for the privilege we have to be
able to come to you; even when we're weary. Thank
you for the rest you speak of that is readily available
when we come to you. I know that my husband carries
burdens that he makes no mention of. I pray that
when he is weary and worn out that your Spirit would
gently remind him that he can come to you. I pray for
a sweet rest to come over my husband even now. I
pray for peace in his mind and that the distractions be
silenced so that he is able to super-naturally rest in
you, even today.

In the name of Jesus, I pray, Amen.

October 18

"Behold, I stand at the door and knock; if anyone hears My voice and opens the door, I will come into him and will dine with him, and he with Me." (Revelation 3:20)

Dear Lord, I continue to lift up my husband to you and pray that he would hear your voice. May he open the door of his heart to you and invite you in, so that he may experience the fullness of your love and grace. Help him to recognize your voice and to discern your plans for his life, even in the midst of confusion or uncertainty. May he never feel alone or abandoned, but instead, constantly feel your presence and comfort. I pray that he would grow in his faith and in his relationship with you, and that he would be a witness to your love and truth. Thank you for your constant pursuit of him and again, for the privilege of praying for my husband.

In the name of Jesus, I pray, Amen.

October 19

*"Holy, holy, holy, is the Lord God Almighty, who was and is and is to come!" **(Revelation 4:8b)***

Dear Lord, I join the heavenly chorus in proclaiming your holiness and glory. You are the Lord God Almighty, who was and is and is to come. You are the Alpha and the Omega, the beginning and the end, and your greatness knows no limits. I am in awe of your power and majesty, grateful for your mercy and love. You alone are worthy of all praise and worship. Almighty God, I pray my husband and our marriage reflect your holiness and grace, and may we always honor you with our thoughts, words, and actions. Thank you for the privilege of knowing you and for the promise of eternal life with you.

In the name of Jesus, I pray, Amen.

October 20

"By day the LORD commands his steadfast love, and at night his song is with me, a prayer to the God of my life."
(Psalm 42:8)

Dear Lord, thank you for being so near, as close as our next breath. You promised never to leave or forsake us, so I pray this for my husband. When he feels alone, surround him with your unfailing love. Lord, you are the creator of life, and we have the privilege of walking with you. I pray he feels your presence today. Command your steadfast love by day and put a song in his heart at night.

In the name of Jesus, I pray, Amen.

October 21

*"I bow down toward your holy temple and give thanks to your name for your steadfast love and your faithfulness, for you have exalted above all things your name and your word." **(Psalm 138:2)***

Dear Lord, I am grateful for your unfailing love and faithfulness. Your faithfulness is great! Today, I lift my husband to you. I pray that he will have a heart of gratitude and devotion as he reflects on your love and faithfulness. Your Name and your Word are exalted above all else. May my husband honor your Name and speak your Word in his words and actions. I pray that he will find strength in worshiping you and feel empowered as he thanks you. Thank you, Lord, for blessing me with a husband who loves to pray and lives to worship you. Thank you, Lord!

In the name of Jesus, I pray, Amen.

October 22

"for the anger of man does not produce the righteousness of God." (James 1:20)

Dear Lord, I ask that my husband's temperament be of peace and not anger. Help him to manage his emotions, resist resentment, pursue righteousness, and avoid wrath. I acknowledge you as a just God who forgives sins. I am grateful for my wonderful husband and pray that he walks in the Spirit, and not in his flesh. May he be rooted in love and peaceful in spirit. Thank you for your powerful presence, and may my husband continue to live a righteous life.

In the name of Jesus, I pray, Amen.

October 23

*"and the Scripture was fulfilled that says, "Abraham be-lieved God, and it was counted to him as righteousness"—and he was called a friend of God." **(James 2:23)***

Dear Lord, I am here to offer my prayer for my husband. You have acknowledged Abraham as your friend because of his faith and obedience, and I humbly ask that my husband follows in his footsteps and becomes your faithful servant. I pray that he may have a heart that trusts and obeys you and always strives to do what is right in your eyes. Additionally, I request your blessings of favor, wisdom, and guidance for him as he navigates through life. Thank you for hearing my prayer.

In the name of Jesus, I pray, Amen.

October 24

"You open your hand; you satisfy the desire of every living thing." (Psalm 145:16)

Dear Lord, thank you for being a God that satisfies the desires of every living thing. Thank you for opening your hand to us. You are our Creator and Provider. I pray for my wonderful husband today and ask that you keep your hand open to him. Because you satisfy his desires, he is fulfilled in you. I pray that you would give him the desires of his heart as he wholeheartedly seeks your face. Quench his thirst, Lord, and may he thirst no more. Fill him with your power and grace. May he pause and ponder on the consistency of your provision in his life.

In the name of Jesus, I pray, Amen.

October 25

*"Know therefore that the LORD your God is God, the faithful God who keeps covenant and steadfast love with those who love him and keep his commandments, to a thousand generations," **(Deuteronomy 7:9)***

Dear God, we praise you for your faithfulness and for being a Promise Keeper. We thank you for keeping your covenant and showering us with your steadfast love because we love you and follow your commandments. Your covenant love extends to a thousand generations, including our children and their children. We receive this promise and I speak it over my husband's life, who loves you and keeps your commandments. May your love guide him all the days of his life.

In the name of Jesus, I pray, Amen.

October 26

"looking to Jesus, the founder and perfecter of our faith, who for the joy that was set before him endured the cross, despising the shame, and is seated at the right hand of the throne of God." (Hebrews 12:2)

Dear God, I am grateful that you endured the cross for us. Today, I ask for your help guiding my husband to focus on you, the author and perfecter of his faith. I pray that he can maintain his focus on you, even when life presents challenges. Please strengthen his faith and grant him the courage to persevere through hardships. I ask that you fill him with your peace, hope, and joy so he can complete the race set before him with endurance. Please help him to let go of anything that hinders his wholehearted devotion to you. May his journey be full of your grace and blessings. Thank you for hearing my prayer, God.

In the name of Jesus, I pray, Amen.

October 27

*"But each person is tempted when he is lured and enticed by his own desire. Then desire when it has conceived gives birth to sin, and sin when it is fully grown brings forth death." **(James 1:14-15)***

Dear God, I am grateful for the gift of my husband today. In this world, there are many temptations. I pray that he remains aware and resists them. May he not be lured by the desires that may lead him toward sin and death. Instead, I pray that he finds true satisfaction and fulfillment in you. Please help him recognize the subtle ways the enemy tempts him and grant him the strength to overcome them. I pray that he confesses and turns away from any sin in his life and experiences the freedom and forgiveness that come from repentance. Please protect him from the destructive consequences of sin and guide him to walk in righteousness and truth. Thank you for your grace and mercy.

In the name of Jesus, I pray, Amen.

October 28

"And they were all filled with the Holy Spirit and began to speak in other tongues as the Spirit gave them utterance." (Acts 2:4)

Dear Lord, thank you for my husband seeking a deeper relationship with you. I pray his thirst for you will be quenched and like on the day of Pentecost, fill our home with the Holy Spirit. Rest on my husband and give him a new heavenly language. Change his life and use him for your glory. Holy Ghost fire, fall! Thank You, Lord.

In the name of Jesus, I pray, Amen.

October 29

*"For you were called to freedom, brothers. Only do not use your freedom as an opportunity for the flesh, but through love serve one another." **(Galatians 5:13)***

Dear God, I am grateful for the freedom you have given us. Today, I pray for my husband not to abuse his liberty in you to satisfy his desires. Please guide him in his spiritual growth and help him to exercise self-control. Instead, may he be led by the Holy Spirit to act out of love and a desire to please you. As he pleases you, I pray that his life is blessed. Make him a servant to others. Thank you for blessing me with a loving husband who strives to put his desires aside for your will.

In the name of Jesus, I pray, Amen.

October 30

*"A sound heart is life to the body, But envy is rottenness to the bones." (**Proverbs 14:30**)*

Dear Lord, I pray for my husband to have a heart that is at peace and free from envy. Help him to be content with what he has and to find joy in the blessings you have given him. Guard his heart against comparing himself to others and feeling inadequate. I pray he celebrates the successes of others and be genuinely happy for their accomplishments. Help him to cultivate a heart of gratitude and humility, and may his life be a testimony of your grace and goodness. I pray he would emanate peace and contentment to those around him. Thank you, Lord, for your love and provision.

In the name of Jesus, I pray, Amen.

October 31

*"Know this, my beloved brothers: let every person be
quick to hear, slow to speak, slow to anger;"*
(James 1:19)

Dear Lord, I bring my husband before you today and
pray that he is quick to listen, slow to speak, and slow
to become angry, just as your word instructs us. Help
him to be a good listener and to truly hear the perspectives and opinions of others. May he be quick to
seek understanding. I ask that you would give him the
wisdom and discernment to respond with grace and
love, even when he doesn't understand. May he be
known for his gentleness, kindness, and patience, and
may his actions reflect the character of Christ. Thank
you for the gift of marriage, Lord, and for the opportunity to grow in love and understanding together.

In the name of Jesus, I pray, Amen.

NOVEMBER

November 1

*"My beloved is to me a cluster of henna blossoms in the vineyards of Engedi." **(Song of Solomon 1:14)***

Dear God, as I pray, I ask that my husband be revitalized and refreshed by the scent of my love. May our love be a pillar of strength and encouragement, reminding him of your love for him. Please guide me to be purposeful in my expressions of love and affection towards him, and may my words and actions serve as a pleasant aroma throughout his life. I pray that he remembers the beauty of our marriage and feels cherished and appreciated. Thank you for bringing us together and for the gift of love. As we grow in our relationship with you, may we always honor and cherish one another.

In the name of Jesus, I pray, Amen.

November 2

"I pray he kiss me with the kisses of his mouth! For your love is sweeter than wine."
(Song of Solomon 1:2)

Dear Lord, I humbly pray for strong love between my husband and me, reflecting your love for us. Please guide us to continually pursue and invest in our relationship, marked by tenderness, affection, and selflessness. I ask for our marriage to be a source of joy and blessings, a testament to your grace and goodness. I thank you for bringing us together, and may our love always bring glory to your Name.

In the name of Jesus, I pray, Amen.

November 3

*"How beautiful you are, my darling, How beautiful you are! Your eyes are like doves." **(Song of Solomon 1:15)***

Dear Lord, I pray that my husband finds me captivating and that he loves and admires me as a precious gift from you. Please help him recognize and appreciate the unique qualities that make me who I am. I pray he is attentive to my needs and desires and provides comfort and support. May our relationship grow and deepen, reflecting your love for us. Thank you for the gift of marriage and the opportunity to experience love and companionship with one another. May our relationship always bring honor to your name.

In the name of Jesus, I pray, Amen.

November 4

"How handsome you are, my beloved, And so delightful!
Indeed, our bed is luxuriant!" **(Song of Solomon 1:16)**

Dear Lord, I am grateful for my attractive husband,
who brings me joy. I am thankful we have a fulfilling
sex life and can experience intimacy in our marriage. I
pray that my husband finds happiness and fulfillment
in our relationship and that it is a source of strength
for him. May our love for each other be a testimony to
your grace and faithfulness, marked by tenderness,
kindness, and mutual respect. Thank you for the gift
of intimacy in marriage and the opportunity to experience the depth of love. I am grateful for your creativity
and appreciate your blessings. Thank you, Lord!

In the name of Jesus, I pray, Amen.

November 5

"I have compared you, my love, to my filly among Pharaoh's chariots." (Song of Solomon 1:9)

Dear God, I humbly request your assistance in helping my husband recognize and cherish the beauty and strength of our relationship, like the admiration expressed by King Solomon towards his lover. I pray that you fill my husband's heart with an appreciation for me and communicating his love and gratitude, rather than being distracted by superficial things. May our marriage bring honor to you and be characterized by beauty, strength, and unfailing love. May we both experience the richness and depth of your affection in our marriage.

In the name of Jesus, I pray, Amen.

November 6

*"The beams of our house are cedars, Our rafters, junipers." (**Song of Solomon 1:17**)*

Dear God, I am grateful that our marriage has a strong foundation and that you are watching over us. I pray that nothing will disrupt our covenant with you and each other. As your Word states, a three-strand cord is not easily broken. I pray that my husband will find comfort and safety in our relationship. May our love be a source of peace and contentment for him, and I pray that we can be there for each other. Please help us be open and supportive of one another. I hope our love for each other reflects your perfect love for us. May we continue to grow in our love for each other and our relationship with you.

In the name of Jesus, I pray, Amen.

November 7

*"Like an apple tree among the trees of the wood, so is my beloved [shepherd] among the sons [cried the girl]! Under his shadow I delighted to sit, and his fruit was sweet to my taste." **(Song of Solomon 2:3)***

Dear God, I am grateful that you chose my husband for me. He is an incredible gift, and I feel honored that you entrusted him to me. Even though I may not understand everything we go through, I trust that you brought us together for a beautiful purpose. I am thankful for the man of God that he is becoming, and I love being around him. I promise to always respect and cherish him as the gift that he is. I am grateful that we can enjoy each other's company and that my husband is sweet. His love is so sweet, and I am appreciative of him. Thank you, Father.

In the name of Jesus, I pray, Amen.

November 8

"He brought me to the banqueting house, and his banner over me was love [for love waved as a protecting and comforting banner over my head when I was near him]."
(Song of Solomon 2:4)

Dear God, I am grateful that my husband loves me unconditionally, just as you love the church. His love provides protection and comfort to me. I pray that he continues to be proud of me as his wife and that we keep investing in our relationship. Let our love be a source of happiness and a haven where we both find solace and rest in each other's company. Thank you for the comfort and security I feel with him. I appreciate having a kind and loving husband.

In the name of Jesus, I pray, Amen.

November 9

"[She said distinctly] My beloved is mine and I am his! He pastures his flocks among the lilies."
(Song of Solomon 2:16)

Dear God, I am grateful for my husband. Thank you for creating us for each other and for the love and commitment we have for one another. I pray that our relationship is strengthened and deepens with each passing day. May my husband always feel loved and cherished by me, and may I always feel the same way about him. I ask that you bless our marriage with beauty, peace, and joy. May my husband find happiness in the simple things in life and be renewed by our connection. Thank you for bringing my soul mate into my life.

In the name of Jesus, I pray, Amen.

November 10

*"You have ravished my heart and given me courage, my sister, my [promised] bride; you have ravished my heart and given me courage with one look from your eyes, with one jewel of your necklace." (**Song of Solomon 4:9**)*

Dear God, Thank you for the gift of love and the beauty of marriage. Please help me support my husband in every possible way and have the strength to encourage him to conquer life's challenges. Please focus my eyes and heart so they echo your love and light. I pray that when my husband looks into my eyes and finds a safe place, he feels a sense of belonging and peace.

In the name of Jesus, I pray, Amen.

November 11

"How beautiful is your love, my sister, my [promised] bride! How much better is your love than wine! And the fragrance of your ointments than all spices!"
(Song of Solomon 4:10)

Dear God, I am grateful for my husband. He brings so much beauty and joy into my life every day. His love is precious to me, better than any wine or spice. I pray he also sees my love as beautiful and appreciates it. Please help me love him unconditionally, just as You love him. May our marriage be strengthened by the love we share. I thank you for my husband and our wonderful friendship. Please bless our marriage and help us grow closer to you and each other every day.

In the name of Jesus, I pray, Amen.

November 12

"[You have called me a garden, she said] Oh, I pray that the [cold] north wind and the [soft] south wind may blow upon my garden, that its spices may flow out [in abundance for you in whom my soul delights]. Let my beloved come into his garden and eat its choicest fruits."
(Song of Solomon 4:16)

Dear Lord, I pray that my husband will come into our garden of love and taste its choice fruits. I ask that you bless our relationship and make it a source of joy and beauty for both of us. May the winds of your Spirit blow upon our garden and spread its fragrance everywhere. May our love be a testimony to your goodness and grace, and may it inspire others to seek after you. I pray that my husband will feel loved and cherished, and that he will find in me a faithful and supportive partner. May he be attracted to what I give and love my fragrance. Thank you for the gift of my husband, and for the love that we share.

In the name of Jesus, I pray, Amen.

November 13

"But Solomon replied, " Like the lily among thorns, so are you, my love, among the daughters."
(Song of Solomon 2:2)

Dear Lord, I am grateful that my husband sees me as a rare and precious lily among thorns. When he sees me, I pray that he sees your goodness and grace in me. Even in a crowded room, I pray he will always recognize my unique beauty. My husband is a shining light in a world that can be dark, and I am thankful for his exceptional qualities. Please continue to bless our marriage and guide us to serve and honor you.

In the name of Jesus, I pray, Amen.

November 14

"Better to be of a humble spirit with the lowly, than to divide the spoil with the proud." **(Proverbs 16:19)**

Dear Lord, your Word declares that it is better to have a humble and lowly spirit, than to be prideful and divide the spoils with the proud. I pray that you will foster a sense of compassion and a willingness to serve others within my husband. I pray for your grace to cultivate a humble spirit in my husband and so that he is mindful of the needs of those who are less fortunate. Give him the strength to resist the temptation of pride and to avoid the pitfalls of selfishness and arrogance. Grant my husband the wisdom to discern what is truly important in life and to prioritize values that honor you and serve others.

In the name of Jesus, I pray, Amen.

November 15

"The one who overcomes, I will grant to him to sit with Me on My throne, as I also overcame and sat with My Father on His throne." **(Revelation 3:21)**

Dear Lord, I pray that my husband will be victorious in his walk and receive the reward promised to the faithful. I pray he is steadfast in his faith, even in the face of trials and temptations. I pray he draws strength and inspiration from your love and grace. Lord, I pray that my husband will sit with you on your throne, just as you were victorious and sat down with your Father on his throne. I pray he experiences the joy and peace that comes from being more than a conqueror in you, and I pray he is becoming a faithful and obedient servant of yours all the days of his life. I pray that he will continue to be rooted in your love and strengthened by your grace.

In the name of Jesus, I pray, Amen.

November 16

"Bless the LORD, O my soul, and forget not all His bene-
*fits:" **(Psalm 103:2)***

Dear Lord, I bless You, O my soul. And with all that is
within me, I bless your holy Name! Father, You forgive all our iniquities, heal all our diseases, redeem
our lives from destruction, and crown us with lovingkindness and tender mercies. You satisfy our
mouths with good things, so that our youth is renewed
like the eagle. Today I declare that Word over my
husband. I declare and decree that You forgive all my
husband's iniquities, You heal all his diseases and
have redeemed his life from destruction. I declare and
decree that You crown my husband with lovingkindness and tender mercies. You satisfy his mouth with
good things and his youth is renewed like the eagle.
What a privilege to serve You! I praise You for the
benefits that come with serving You. Bless his life,
Lord. I pray this prayer with confidence.

In the name of Jesus, I pray, Amen.

November 17

"Lead me in Your truth and teach me, for You are the God
of my salvation: On You I wait all the day."
(Psalm 25:5)

Dear Lord, as I continue to bring my beloved husband before you, I pray that you would lead him in your truth and teach him. Your truth brings life and clarity. Your truth dissolves darkness. Thank you for your truth! You are the God of our salvation. I pray that my husband continues to make you the God of his salvation. May he position himself to wait all day for you. May he find fulfillment in the truth of your word. Thank you for saving him and changing his life. May he continue to grow in your truth and I pray that he allows your truth to carve out areas in his life that don't align with your Word. I pray that you get the glory out of his life.

In the name of Jesus, I pray, Amen.

November 18

"Ah, Lord GOD! Behold, You have made the heavens and the earth by Your great power and outstretched arm. There is nothing too hard for You." **(Jeremiah 32:17)**

Dear Lord, as the Creator of all things, the heavens, and the earth, I acknowledge nothing is too hard for you. I praise you for your sovereignty and eternal reign. Today, I humbly request that you remind my husband of your limitless power and that he may trust in your abilities during challenging times. I pray you bless him with the faith and courage to rely on your goodness. May he continue to build a stronger relationship with you and be strengthened by your Spirit. I ask that he becomes a man of prayer and devotion, seeking your will in all circumstances.

In the name of Jesus, I pray, Amen.

November 19

"And those who know Your name will put their trust in You; For You, LORD, have not forsaken those who seek You." (Psalm 9:10)

Dear Lord, I pray that my husband will know your Name and trust in you completely. May he be reminded that you have never forsaken those who seek you, and that you are always with him, even in the darkest of times. I ask that you would bless him with a deep and abiding faith, and that he would be confident in your love and goodness. I pray that my husband will seek you in all things, and that he will be guided by your wisdom and understanding. Thank you for the gift of my husband, and for the love and grace that you have shown to us both. I pray that our marriage will continue to be rooted in your love and strengthened by your grace. I put my trust in You.

In the name of Jesus, I pray, Amen.

November 20

*"Do not lie to one another, since you have put off the old man with his deeds, and have put on the new man who is renewed in knowledge according to the image of Him who created him," **(Colossians 3:9-10)***

Dear Lord, today I ask for your help in strengthening my marriage. I pray we can always be honest and approach one another with kindness and love. Please guide us with your truth. Renew our commitment. I pray we can communicate honestly and have the courage to share our hearts and struggles. Please help us to understand each other's perspectives and to listen with empathy and compassion. As we walk with you, may we always be grateful for one another and grow deeper in love.

In the name of Jesus, I pray, Amen.

November 21

*"He who has an ear, let him hear what the Spirit says to the churches." **(Revelation 3:22)***

Dear God, I am praying for my husband today. Please help him to hear what the Spirit is saying to him. May he be sensitive to your guidance and obedient to your will. I ask that he listens for your voice in every aspect of his life and seeks your wisdom above all else. Please help him to be open to your leadership and willing to follow wherever you call him. Please continue to fill him with your Spirit and guide him on his journey. I pray that he becomes a man of prayer and devotion, seeking your face with all his heart. Thank you for hearing my prayer.

In the name of Jesus, I pray, Amen.

November 22

"The LORD will open to you His good treasure, the heavens, to give the rain to your land in its season, and to bless all the work of your hand. You shall lend to many nations, but you shall not borrow."
(Deuteronomy 28:12)

Dear Lord, my prayer is for my husband to achieve financial prosperity and success. I ask for your blessings to be poured upon him, creating opportunities for abundance and wealth in his life. I pray that you grant him the wisdom and guidance he needs to make sound financial decisions and to be a good steward of his resources. As promised in your word, I pray that he will lend to many nations but never need to borrow. Thank you for the blessings you have already bestowed upon him, and I pray that you will continue to guide him in all things and bring him joy and contentment in your provision.

In the name of Jesus, I pray, Amen.

November 23

"May you be blessed by the LORD, who made heaven and earth." (Psalm 115:15)

Dear God, Creator of the heavens and the earth, I am here to pray for my husband's friendships. Please bless him with great relationships that bring him joy, encouragement, and support. You have designed us to live in community with one another, and I ask that my husband finds deep and meaningful friendships. Please help him be a good friend to others and invest in the relationships that matter most. Protect him from harmful friendships and give him discernment and wisdom when choosing who to spend time with. Thank you for my husband and the ways you have blessed him. I pray that he continues to experience your goodness and grace in his friendships and always gives thanks for your many blessings.

In the name of Jesus, I pray, Amen.

November 24

"being confident of this very thing, that He who has begun a good work in you will complete it until the day of Jesus Christ;" **(Philippians 1:6)**

Dear Lord, I pray that my husband will have faith in your power and goodness to complete the good work you have started in him. I trust you have a plan and purpose for his life and all things for his benefit. May he trust that you can change and mold him to be more like you. I am grateful for how you have worked in his life and the many ways you will continue to do so. Please help him grow in his relationship with you and become the man you want him to be. Thank you for always being faithful in his life.

In the name of Jesus, I pray, Amen.

November 25

*"If any of you lacks wisdom, let him ask of God, who gives to all liberally and without reproach, and it will be given to him." **(James 1:5)***

Dear God, I appreciate the blessing of wisdom you provide when we ask for it. Today, I pray for my husband to seek your guidance in all aspects of his life. As a husband, father, son, and brother, he faces numerous challenges and decisions daily, and he needs your assistance to navigate them. I pray he approaches you with an open and humble heart, seeking the wisdom only you can provide. Additionally, I would like to thank you for the gift of my husband and your faithfulness in his life. I pray that he continues to grow in his relationship with you and becomes the man you have called him to be.

In the name of Jesus, I pray, Amen.

November 26

*"For You, O LORD, will bless the righteous; With favor You will surround him as with a shield." **(Psalm 5:12)***

Dear God, I am grateful for the blessings and favor you bestow upon those who seek to live righteously and follow your ways. Today, I pray for my husband to lead a godly life filled with integrity and honor, always striving to do what is right and pleasing to you. I also pray he strengthens his relationship with you and fully embraces your grace. May your blessings and favor be with him today and always.

In the name of Jesus, I pray, Amen.

November 27

"I will love You, O Lord, my strength. The Lord is my rock and my fortress and my deliverer; My God, my strength, in whom I will trust; My shield and the horn of my salvation, my stronghold." **(Psalm 18:1-2)**

Dear God, I am grateful for being able to rely on you to be my husband's rock, fortress, and deliverer. I pray that he always finds refuge in you and feels your love and strength within him. Please help him trust in you and rely on your strength, which is made perfect in his weakness. I ask that you remind him of the depth of your love for him and that he knows he is never alone.

I trust in your unfailing love and faithfulness, and I know that you will always be there for my husband, as you are always there for me. You are my strength, and I love you.

In the name of Jesus, I pray, Amen.

November 28

"For [if we are] in Christ Jesus neither circumcision nor uncircumcision means anything, but only faith activated and expressed and working through love."
(Galatians 5:6)

Dear Lord, I want to express my gratitude for my husband, a precious gift from you. As I pray for him, I am reminded of the truth in your word; the only thing that counts is faith expressing itself through love. I pray that his faith in you would continue to grow and deepen with each passing day. May he come to know you more intimately and experience the fullness of your love in his life. Lord, I pray that my husband's faith would be expressed through love in all that he does. I thank you that my husband is not too focused on outward practices or religious rules, but that his heart is fully devoted to you. May his faith in you be the driving force behind his actions, and may his love for others be a natural outpouring of that faith.

In the name of Jesus, I pray, Amen.

November 29

"This poor man cried, and the LORD heard him and saved him from all his troubles." **(Psalm 34:6)**

Dear Lord, I am grateful for your attention to our needs. I pray that my husband will turn to you for help during difficult times and trust that you can rescue him from any trouble. I hope he can find solace and power in your embrace. Father, I pray that my husband will have an enduring belief in you. Thank you for hearing our prayers and protecting us from all difficulties. May my husband recognize the extent of your love for him and trust you throughout his life.

In the name of Jesus, I pray, Amen.

November 30

*"but the L*ORD *takes pleasure in those who fear him, in those who hope in his steadfast love." (Psalm 147:11)*

Dear Lord, Thank you for the gift of my husband, and I pray that you will continue to watch over him and protect him each and every day. I pray that my husband will always have a deep reverence and respect for you, Lord, and that he will put his hope and trust in your unfailing love. May he find joy and comfort in knowing that you delight in him and that he is always in your loving care. I pray that you will guide him and lead him on the path that you have set out for him.

Lord, I ask that you bless my husband with good health, peace of mind, and a joyful heart. May he feel your presence with him today and always.

In the name of Jesus, I pray, Amen.

DECEMBER

December 1

"Praise the LORD! Praise the LORD from the heavens;
*praise him in the heights!" **(Psalm 148:1)***

Dear Lord, on this first day of December, I want to offer a prayer of praise to You, Lord. You are the Creator of all things, and everything that exists was created by Your hand. I praise You for Your love and mercy that never fail, and for Your faithfulness that endures forever. Your grace is abundant, and You are worthy of all honor, glory, and praise. Your power and majesty are evident in the beauty of the world around me, from the mountains and seas to the stars and sun. I thank You for the gift of life and the blessings You have given me and my husband. Your love never ends, and I pray that I will always remember to give You the praise and adoration You deserve. May our lives and marriage reflect Your goodness and bring honor and glory to Your name.

In the name of Jesus, I pray, Amen.

December 2

"Every good gift and every perfect gift is from above, coming down from the Father of lights, with whom there is no variation or shadow due to change." **(James 1:17)**

Dear Lord, I express my gratitude for my beloved husband, who is an incredible gift from You. I am thankful for the many ways he enriches my life and the lives of those around him. Please guide and direct him in all that he does. Help him to acknowledge that all good things come from You and instill in him a heart of gratitude and thankfulness. Help me to always see him as the perfect gift You have given me from above. My prayer is that he will continue to deepen his relationship with You each day, and that his connection with You will be the foundation of his life. May he find joy and fulfillment in serving You. Thank You, Lord, for my husband and all the good and perfect gifts that come from You.

In the name of Jesus, I pray, Amen.

December 3

"But I have this against you, that you have left your first love." (Revelation 2:4)

Dear Lord, as my husband's partner in faith, I pray he will never forget the love he first had for You. May his love for You only grow stronger with time and may he never stray from Your path. I pray that he will always remember the joy and excitement he felt when he first began his journey with You. May his heart be filled with passion for You, burning with love and devotion. Lord, please keep my husband safe from any temptation that may lead him away from his first love. Protect his heart, mind, and soul, and keep him rooted in Your love. I pray that my husband will always honor and glorify You in everything he does. Thank You for the gift of my husband and his love for You. May his love for You continue to flourish and grow.

In the name of Jesus, I pray, Amen.

December 4

"But the meek shall inherit the land and delight them-selves in abundant peace." ***(Psalm 37:11)***

Dear Lord, I pray that my husband will possess meek-ness, humility, and gentleness. I declare and decree that he will find peace and prosperity in You instead of the things of this world. Please guide him on the path of righteousness and help him make wise choices that honor You. May he be a man of integrity and honor, and always strive to do what is right in your sight.

Lord, I ask that You bless my husband with good health, strength, vitality, and abundant peace. May he continue to walk in Your ways and inherit the land of eternal life that You have prepared for him.

In the name of Jesus, I pray, Amen.

December 5

*"And I will make them and the places all around my hill a blessing, and I will send down the showers in their season; they shall be showers of blessing." (**Ezekiel 34:26**)*

Dear Lord, I thank You for the power in your Word. I declare and decree that You will make my husband a blessing. I pray he is a blessing to everyone he encounters. Thank You for pouring out showers of blessings upon my husband's life in this season. Lord, I ask that You bless my husband with financial prosperity and stability. Provide for his every need and bless the work of his hands. Thank you for the gift of my husband, the ways that he blesses me, our marriage, and our family. I pray he continues to walk in your ways and be a source of blessings to all those around him.

In the name of Jesus, I pray, Amen.

December 6

"Consider it nothing but joy, my brothers and sisters,
whenever you fall into various trials. Be assured that the
testing of your faith [through experience] produces en-
durance [leading to spiritual maturity, and inner peace].
And let endurance have its perfect result and do a thor-
ough work, so that you may be perfect and completely
developed [in your faith], lacking in nothing."
(James 1:2-4)

Dear Lord, I come before You today to lift up my husband in prayer. I ask that You strengthen his faith and
help him to remain steadfast in his devotion to You.
Thank You for being with him, even when he walks
through the valley of the shadow of death. Remind
him that the testing of his faith produces endurance
and spiritual maturity. I ask that You bless him with
peace and contentment, and that You use his trials to
advance your kingdom here on earth. Continue to do
a work in him, Lord, so that he may be completely developed, lacking nothing.

In the name of Jesus, I pray, Amen.

December 7

"But the righteous shall be glad; they shall exult before God; they shall be jubilant with joy!" **(Psalm 68:3)**

Dear Lord, I come before you today with a grateful heart for the gift of my husband. I pray that you would bless him and keep him, and that your face would shine upon him. May you grant him strength and courage as he goes about his tasks today, and may he always know the depth of your love for him. Thank You for a righteous husband. I pray that he would experience the joy and happiness that comes from knowing and walking with You. Thank you for the wonderful man that he is, the man he is becoming, and for the ways that he has blessed my life. May he be jubilant with joy all the days of his life.

In the name of Jesus, I pray, Amen.

December 8

"For if these qualities are yours and are increasing, they keep you from being ineffective or unfruitful in the knowledge of our Lord Jesus Christ." (2 Peter 1:8)

Dear Lord, I come to You in prayer for my beloved husband. I ask that You help him to develop and strengthen his faith, virtue, knowledge, self-control, steadfastness, godliness, brotherly affection, and love. Please allow these qualities to evolve within him each day and help him to become more like You in every aspect. Lord, I pray that my husband can utilize his abilities and talents to serve You and become fruitful in his knowledge of You. May his life reflect Your love and grace. I also pray that You guide him in all his endeavors and continue to bless his work. I pray that his faith continues to grow and that he can be a shining example of Your love in this world.

In the name of Jesus, I pray, Amen.

December 9

"For God is not a God of confusion but of peace."
(1 Corinthians 14:33a)

Dear Lord, I express my gratitude for the precious gift of marriage. I humbly ask that You remain the foundation of our marriage and guide us in seeking Your will for our lives. You are a God of peace, not confusion, so I ask that You fill our marriage with peace and help us to communicate in a way that uplifts and strengthens our bond. May Your love flow through us, and may we always be willing to forgive, slow to anger, and serve each other with selflessness and humility. May we honor and cherish each other and prioritize the needs of the other. Thank You, God, for the love and gift of marriage. I pray that our marriage will always reflect Your love and grace, and that we will continue to grow together in our journey with You.

In the name of Jesus, I pray, Amen.

December 10

"Seek the Lord *while he may be found; call upon him while he is near;" **(Isaiah 55:6)***

Dear Lord, I am thankful that You are always there for us and that we can turn to You whenever we need to. You are the Almighty God, yet You still choose to stay close to us and be present in our lives. Father, I ask for Your help today as I pray for my husband. I want him to draw closer to You and experience Your love and grace in his life. Please give him a strong desire to seek You while You are near and reveal Your truth to him as he does so. Guide him in all his endeavors and bless him with wisdom, discernment, and understanding. May he always uphold righteousness and integrity, finding peace and rest in Your presence. Thank You for my husband and the many ways in which he enriches my life.

In the name of Jesus, I pray, Amen.

December 11

*"I will remember the deeds of the LORD; yes, I will re-member your wonders of old." **(Psalm 77:11)***

Dear Lord, today I pray that my husband remembers the wonders and works that You have done in his life. May he find strength in reflecting on Your faithfulness and be inspired in his own faith. Please bring him comfort and peace, knowing that You have kept, protected, and blessed him throughout his life. May he never forget the big and small miracles that You have performed for him. I pray that he continues to worship You for who You are. Continue to bless him with good health, happiness, and success in all of his endeavors.

In the name of Jesus, I pray, Amen.

December 12

"We ought always to give thanks to God for you, brothers and sisters, as is only fitting, because your faith is increasing abundantly, and the love of each and every one of you toward one another grows ever greater."

(2 Thessalonians 1:3)

Dear Lord, I lift my husband to You today and give thanks for him, just as it says in Your word. Help me to always give thanks for my husband. Lord, I thank You for the ways that his faith is growing and that it positively impacts our marriage. Strengthen the love within him and the love he shows to me and others so that when anyone leaves his presence, they are made better because they experience the love of Christ through him.

In the name of Jesus, I pray, Amen.

December 13

*"Therefore humble yourselves under the mighty hand of God, that He may exalt you in due time, casting all your care upon Him, for He cares for you." (**1 Peter 5:6-7**)*

Dear Lord, I thank you that my husband humbles himself daily under your mighty hand. I thank You that Your word says You may exalt him in due time. I praise You for blessing me with a man that takes up his cross daily. Give him the capacity to endure until that time comes. Thank You that he knows to cast all his cares upon You because you care. Thank You for loving and caring for my husband, your son, the way You do. Lord, you are so good. And we are so undeserving. I pray he rests in the truth that You truly care for him. Remind him that he doesn't need to appear mighty as the world would define, but that he is strong in You.

In the name of Jesus, I pray, Amen.

December 14

"Flee the evil desires of youth and pursue righteousness, faith, love, and peace, along with those who call on the Lord out of a pure heart." **(2 Timothy 2:22)**

Dear Lord, thank You for my husband, a mature man of faith who chases after You, pursuing righteousness, faith, love, and peace. Give him the strength to flee the desires of his youth as they continue to entice him. I pray he joins with those who call on You out of a pure heart. If there be any wicked way in his heart, I pray that You would reveal it. Give him the strength and humility to confess it, repent and continue his pursuit of righteousness. I declare and decree that my husband is free from the desires of his old nature and that he now clings to You. Fill his cup, Lord.

In the name of Jesus, I pray, Amen.

December 15

*"For I know the plans that I have for you,' declares the Lord, 'plans for prosperity and not for disaster, to give you a future and a hope." **(Jeremiah 29:11)***

Lord, I thank You that You knew my husband before he was in his mother's womb. Thank You that all things in his life have worked and are working together for good because he is called according to your purpose. Thank You for the plans that You have for him, plans for prosperity, and plans to give him a future and hope. I thank You Lord for including me in that plan! I pray he walks in confidence knowing that You have everything worked out. Thank you for using his life to bless others. Thank you for making him prosperous. Thank you for his future and thank you that our future is in your hands. I trust you. And Lord, increase his hope. Teach him to always love, always trust, and to always hope.

In the name of Jesus, I pray, Amen.

December 16

*"Then you will call upon Me and come and pray to Me,
and I will listen to you. And you will seek Me and find Me
when you search for Me with all your heart."*
(Jeremiah 29: 12-13)

Dear Lord, As I pray for him, I thank You that my
husband is a man of prayer. I thank You that he seeks
You and searches for You with all his heart. Thank
You for hearing his prayers. Tend to his mind, will
and emotions. Wash them through the Holy Spirit. I
am so grateful that he knows who to call upon and
who to come to for his needs. Let him not look to me,
or other temporal things to fulfill his needs, but Lord
let him look to You. And Lord if he is searching for
anything else outside of You, gently remind him that
You are all he needs. I thank You for my amazing
husband and I praise You that he is fearfully and
wonderfully made.

In the name of Jesus, I pray, Amen.

December 17

"I will let Myself be found by you,' declares the Lord, 'and I will restore your fortunes and gather you from all the nations and all the places where I have driven you,' declares the Lord, 'and I will bring you back to the place from where I sent you into exile."

(Jeremiah 29: 14)

Dear Lord, I praise You for my husband and for the love and blessings that he brings to my life. Thank you that my husband can find you when he is lost and that he has found you. Thank You for calling him out of his past, leading and guiding him in Your ways. I pray that as he follows you, my husband will experience restoration in all areas of his life, and he will be a testament to your restoring power. I pray that You would give him the strength and courage to persevere through difficult times. I pray he finds hope and peace in your presence and trust in your plan for his life.

In the name of Jesus, I pray, Amen.

December 18

*"Enlarge the place of your tent; Stretch out the curtains of your dwellings, do not spare them; Lengthen your ropes. And strengthen your pegs." **(Isaiah 54:2)***

Dear Lord, I thank You for the opportunity to expand in You. I pray for my husband today that You would enlarge his territory. Enlarge the place of his tent. Let everything that he touches prosper. Expand his hopes and dreams. Give him the gift of faith to dream bigger. Stir up your Spirit in him to begin to make room for your blessings. Let him not be afraid or feel inadequate. Encourage his spirit to start preparing for what You have created him for. And use me Lord to nurture the gifts that are in him. Empower us to establish a firm foundation, saturated in You, as we build a legacy for our children and for generations to come.

In the name of Jesus, I pray, Amen.

December 19

"Behold, I will do a new thing, now it shall spring forth; shall you not know it? I will even make a road in the wilderness and rivers in the desert." **(Isaiah 43:19)**

Dear Lord, today I come with a heart filled with gratitude and hope for my husband. I ask that you manifest this promise to do a new thing in my husband's life today. Open new doors for him, providing opportunities that exceed his expectations. Make a way where there seems to be no way, leading him through the wilderness of challenges and uncertainties. Let your refreshing streams of wisdom, provision, and favor quench his thirst and nourish his soul. Grant him strength, resilience, and discernment to navigate every desert season he encounters. Remind him that you are the God who performs miracles and makes a way where there is no way.

In the name of Jesus, I pray, Amen.

December 20

"When you pass through the waters, I will be with you; And through the rivers, they will not overflow you. When you walk through the fire, you will not be scorched, nor will the flame burn you." **(Isaiah 43:2)**

Dear Lord, thank You for your word that says you will be with us as we pass through the waters. Be with my husband as he goes through tough and turbulent times. Overwhelm him with your Presence so he is certain that You are always there. I know life circumstances may try to overtake him, but remind him that he will not drown. As he walks through the fire, I pray that the Holy Spirit will remind him of the three Hebrew boys who were not even cinched in the fire. Thank you for preserving him. You are such a faithful God and your promises are true! Hallelujah to your Name!

In the name of Jesus, I pray, Amen.

December 21

"But now, this is what the Lord says, He who is your Cre-
ator, Jacob, And He who formed you, Israel: "Do not
fear, for I have redeemed you; I have called you by name;
*you are Mine!" **(Isaiah 43:1)***

Dear Lord, I thank You that You have called my husband by name and that he is yours! You created him.
You formed him. The hairs on his head are
numbered. So Father I pray that You would remove
fear from his heart and soul. Help him to remember
that You are his redeemer and his savior. Come close,
God. Like the warmth from the sun on a beautiful
day, may he bask in your redeeming love. You're such
a good, good Father.

In the name of Jesus, I pray, Amen.

December 22

"Do not turn to the right or the left; Remove your foot from evil." ***(Proverbs 4:27)***

Dear Lord, I pray for my husband that he not swerve to the right or to the left. May his feet be firmly planted on the path of righteousness. I pray that You would give him the wisdom and discernment to make wise decisions and to avoid anything that would lead him astray. Help him to keep his eyes fixed on You, and to trust in your guidance and provision for his life. May my husband be a light in this world, shining your truth and goodness to those around him. I pray that he has the courage to stand firm in his faith, even when it's unpopular. May he continue to grow in his relationship with You, and may his life be a testimony to your goodness and faithfulness.

In the name of Jesus, I pray, Amen.

December 23

"This Book of the Law shall not depart from your mouth, but you shall meditate in it day and night, that you may observe to do according to all that is written in it. For then you will make your way prosperous, and then you will have good success." **(Joshua 1:8)**

Dear Lord, thank You that my husband is a man who passionately observes the word, speaks the word, and lives the word. Do not let the Book of the Law depart from his mouth. Lord, let him lead our family to also observe all that is written. I declare and decree that together we will meditate on Your word. In doing so, you will make our way prosperous. We will have good success in our faith, family, and finances.

In the name of Jesus, I pray, Amen.

December 24

*"I do not pray for these alone, but also for those who will
believe in Me through their word; that they all may be
one, as You, Father, are in Me, and I in You; that they
also may be one in Us, that the world may believe that
You sent Me. And the glory which You gave Me I have
given them, that they may be one just as We are one: I in
them, and You in Me; that they may be made perfect in
one, and that the world may know that You have sent Me,
and have loved them as You have loved Me."*

(John 17: 20-23)

Dear Lord, As I come before you today, I pray that my
husband may be one with You, as You are one with Jesus Christ. I pray that he would be rooted in your love
and guided by your wisdom, and that he would seek to
honor you in all that he does. Lord, I ask that you
would protect him from the schemes of the enemy and
keep him from all harm. I pray that if my husband is
not one with You, that You would direct his heart back
to you. I pray that your light would begin to shine
again through him and that your glory would rest on
his. Make him know the love You have for him as his

Father. Touch his heart, like only You can. May he be secure in you. Lord, I pray that You would bring unity and harmony in our marriage, as we seek to grow closer to You and to each other. May we be a reflection of your love and truth to those around us, and may our marriage be a source of strength and encouragement to others.

In the name of Jesus, I pray, Amen.

December 25

*"Who is wise and understanding among you? Let them show it by their good life, by deeds done in the humility that comes from wisdom." (**James 3:13**)*

Dear Lord, I want to begin this prayer by wishing a very happy birthday to Jesus. Thank you for sending your only son to the world to grant us eternal life. Your wisdom is unmatched, and I am grateful for your guidance. On this Christmas holiday, I pray for my husband's well-being. I am thankful that he seeks wisdom and understanding, and his good deeds are done with humility instead of pride. He is an exemplary man, and I thank you for him. Please help me to appreciate the good in him, even when I forget or take it for granted. I am grateful for the gift of my husband, and I pray for his continued happiness and success.

In the name of Jesus, I pray, Amen.

December 26

"I am using an example from everyday life because of your human limitations. Just as you used to offer yourselves as slaves to impurity and to ever-increasing wickedness, so now offer yourselves as slaves to righteousness leading to holiness." (Romans 6:19)

Dear Lord, I thank and praise You that my husband is no longer a slave to impurity and ever-increasing wickedness. Thank you for calling him out of darkness and that now he is a slave to righteousness, being sanctified day by day. Thank you for changing his life and saving his soul. Lord, I ask that You would guide my husband as he seeks to obey your commands and live out your will for his life. I pray that he would be filled with your Spirit, and that your love would overflow from him to others. I pray that You would continue to work in his heart and transform him into the image of your Son, Jesus Christ.

In the name of Jesus, I pray, Amen.

December 27

"May you be filled with joy." (Colossians 9:11b)

Dear Lord, my request today for my husband is simple. I ask that he be filled with joy. If there are any past or present life events that have caused him pain or resentment, I pray that you will help him find the root of these issues and heal him from the inside out. I believe that his joy will be complete if he turns to You, and that the Joy of the Lord will become his strength.

In the name of Jesus, I pray, Amen.

December 28

"For though we live in the world, we do not wage war as the world does. The weapons we fight with are not the weapons of the world. On the contrary, they have divine power to demolish strongholds."
(2 Corinthians 10:3-4)

Dear Lord, I thank you for a husband that uses spiritual weapons to wage war and to demolish strongholds. Thank you that he is not reactive, but rather, proactive in spiritual matters. I thank You that my husband understands how to engage spiritually. Lead him to operate in Your divine power to break chains in his life; casting down imaginations and every high thing that exalts itself against the knowledge of God. May he bring into captivity every thought to the obedience of Christ.

In the name of Jesus, I pray, Amen.

December 29

"so that you may become blameless and pure, "children of God without fault in a warped and crooked generation."
Then you will shine among them like stars in the sky."
(Philippians 2:15)

Dear Lord, I thank You for my awesome husband. I lift him up to You knowing that this world and society are warped and crooked. I pray that You will continue to nurture my husband so that he becomes blameless and pure in You. With so many worldly influences prevalent, I pray that You would guide his heart back to the things of You. I thank You Lord that it is possible to walk blameless in this world because of the power of the Holy Spirit. I pray that You would lift up a standard around my husband. Give him confidence to operate and walk in the Spirit. Let him shine among others with your light.

In the name of Jesus, I pray, Amen.

December 30

"Take my yoke upon you. Let me teach you, because I am humble and gentle at heart, and you will find rest for your souls. For my yoke is easy to bear, and the burden I give you is light." **(Matthew 11: 29-30)**

Dear Lord, I pray that because You are humble and gentle at heart, You would do as your word says and teach my husband. Teach him how to be a loving husband, father and friend. Heavenly Father, only You know how to speak to his heart. Whatever method You use to speak to him, I pray his heart is softened to receive the lesson. May he find rest for his soul where there may be uncertainty or confusion. Thank You for the burden that You give, which is light - in comparison to everything the world has to offer. Let him release those things that hold him captive and grab a hold to your yoke, which is easy to bear. Give him rest for his weary soul.

In the name of Jesus, I pray, Amen.

December 31

*"Be faithful until death, and I will give you the crown of life." **(Revelation 2:10b)***

Dear Lord, thank You for placing the desire in me to pray for my husband every day of this year. On this last day of the year, as I conclude this book of prayers for my beloved husband, I pray that you would grant him the perseverance to finish out this year strong. Give him the strength he needs to begin the new year with a spirit of excellence. Help him to be faithful until death and to stay focused and diligent with what lies ahead. Thank You for keeping him through the year and I pray that in the new year he will be faithful in everything he sets out to do. Guide him with your wisdom and inspire him through the Holy Spirit. Lord, You are faithful. Thank You for being everything we need.

In the name of Jesus, I pray, Amen.

Final Prayer of Agreement

Dear Lord, Thank You for the privilege to come to You daily on my husband's behalf and speak life over him. Thank you for the gift to commune with You and the partnership I have with You to bless my husband. I am grateful for all the wives who have remained faithful in their commitment to pray for their current or future husbands. May Your will be fulfilled in their lives, their husbands' lives, and in their marriages, just as it is in heaven. I pray that their marriages are firm and will flourish with love. Father, I ask that their unwavering devotion results in positive and permanent transformations in their lives. I pray this prayer in the Mighty Name of Jesus Christ and touch and agree with every sister on earth, praying these 365 prayers over their husbands and future husbands.

In the name of Jesus, I pray, Amen.